DATE DUE

			PRINTED IN U.S.A.

1st EDITION

Perspectives on Diseases and Disorders

Ovarian Cancer

Christina Fisanick
Book Editor

GALE
CENGAGE Learning

Detroit • New York • San Francisco • New Haven, Conn • Waterville, Maine • London

Elizabeth Des Chenes, *Director, Publishing Solutions*

For more information, contact:
Greenhaven Press
27500 Drake Rd.
Farmington Hills, MI 48331-3535
Or you can visit our Internet site at gale.cengage.com

For product information and technology assistance, contact us at

Gale Customer Support, 1-800-877-4253
For permission to use material from this text or product, submit all requests online at www.cengage.com/permissions

Further permissions questions can be e-mailed to permissionrequest@cengage.com

Articles in Greenhaven Press anthologies are often edited for length to meet page requirements. In addition, original titles of these works are changed to clearly present the main thesis and to explicitly indicate the author's opinion. Every effort is made to ensure that Greenhaven Press accurately reflects the original intent of the authors. Every effort has been made to trace the owners of copyrighted material.

Cover image © Medical Body Scans/Photo Researchers, Inc./Getty Images

LIBRARY OF CONGRESS CATALOGING-IN-PUBLICATION DATA

Ovarian cancer / Christina Fisanick, book editor.
   p. cm. -- (Perspectives on diseases and disorders)
Includes bibliographical references and index.
ISBN 978-0-7377-5781-1 (hardcover)
1. Ovaries--Cancer. I. Fisanick, Christina.
  RC280.O8O86 2012
  616.99'465--dc23

                                       2012012539

Printed in the United States of America
1 2 3 4 5 6 7 16 15 14 13 12

CONTENTS

FOREWORD

"Medicine, to produce health, has to examine disease."
—Plutarch

Independent research on a health issue is often the first step to complement discussions with a physician. But locating accurate, well-organized, understandable medical information can be a challenge. A simple Internet search on terms such as "cancer" or "diabetes," for example, returns an intimidating number of results. Sifting through the results can be daunting, particularly when some of the information is inconsistent or even contradictory. The Greenhaven Press series Perspectives on Diseases and Disorders offers a solution to the often overwhelming nature of researching diseases and disorders.

From the clinical to the personal, titles in the Perspectives on Diseases and Disorders series provide students and other researchers with authoritative, accessible information in unique anthologies that include basic information about the disease or disorder, controversial aspects of diagnosis and treatment, and first-person accounts of those impacted by the disease. The result is a well-rounded combination of primary and secondary sources that, together, provide the reader with a better understanding of the disease or disorder.

Each volume in Perspectives on Diseases and Disorders explores a particular disease or disorder in detail. Material for each volume is carefully selected from a wide range of sources, including encyclopedias, journals, newspapers, nonfiction books, speeches, government documents, pamphlets, organization newsletters, and position papers. Articles in the first chapter provide an authoritative, up-to-date overview that covers symptoms, causes and effects, treatments, cures, and medical advances. The second chapter presents a substantial number of opposing viewpoints on controversial treatments and other current debates relating to the volume topic. The third chapter offers a variety of personal perspectives on the disease or disorder. Patients, doctors, caregivers, and loved ones represent just some of the voices found in this narrative chapter.

Each Perspectives on Diseases and Disorders volume also includes:

- An **annotated table of contents** that provides a brief summary of each article in the volume.
- An **introduction** specific to the volume topic.
- Full-color **charts and graphs** to illustrate key points, concepts, and theories.
- Full-color **photos** that show aspects of the disease or disorder and enhance textual material.
- **"Fast Facts"** that highlight pertinent additional statistics and surprising points.
- A **glossary** providing users with definitions of important terms.
- A **chronology** of important dates relating to the disease or disorder.
- An annotated list of **organizations to contact** for students and other readers seeking additional information.
- A **bibliography** of additional books and periodicals for further research.
- A detailed **subject index** that allows readers to quickly find the information they need.

Whether a student researching a disorder, a patient recently diagnosed with a disease, or an individual who simply wants to learn more about a particular disease or disorder, a reader who turns to Perspectives on Diseases and Disorders will find a wealth of information in each volume that offers not only basic information, but also vigorous debate from multiple perspectives.

INTRODUCTION

Despite advances in detection and treatment, ovarian cancer remains the leading cause of gynecologic cancer death in the United States. Although the disease is easily treatable, no cure exists. Of those women who survive beyond five years, few make it five more. In fact, pathology researchers at Johns Hopkins Medical Center estimate that 70 to 90 percent of patients with ovarian cancer will suffer from at least one recurrence. Understandably, coping with a deadly disease that returns again and again presents a host of problems for patients.

Few women know of these trials more than Elizabeth McLeod, who details her story on the ovarian cancer page of the Johns Hopkins Pathology website. In her essay, dated November 1, 2011, she details her battle with the deadly disease. In many ways her struggle is similar to many other women who have fought ovarian cancer, including the way it was discovered, the cancer stage at original diagnosis, and the multiple recurrences. Throughout the past decade, she has fought the disease and attempted to cope with all of the emotional turmoil and physical pain it has brought into her life.

McLeod's ovarian cancer was diagnosed during emergency surgery for what she thought was an abdominal infection from a burst appendix. The surgeons stopped the surgery early when they discovered tumors instead. She was diagnosed with stage III cancer, which means that the disease had spread to other organs as well. According to the American Cancer Society's *Cancer Facts & Figures 2011*, if the disease is caught before it spreads to other organs, 94 percent of women will be alive five years after diagnosis. Unfortunately, only 15 percent of all cases of ovarian cancer are caught at the localized stage. Stage III and IV ovarian cancer patients can expect a five-year survival rate of 73 percent and 28 percent, respectively, due in part to the disease's tendency to recur.

Doctors immediately went to work treating McLeod's cancer. As she writes, "After a complete debulking and six rounds of Taxol/Carboplatin [chemotherapy drugs] I finally went into remission . . . if you can actually do that with this type of cancer." In other words, following months of treatment, she was finally given the "no existing disease" (NED) declaration. In a September 3, 2002, article in the *Pittsburgh Post-Gazette*, staff writer Betsy Kline reflects on the NED diagnosis. She states, "Dancing with NED is the feeling of renewed vigor after months of chemotherapy-induced nausea and fatigue. It's the feel of the wind in a new growth of hair and a spring in feet that were once numb." Regrettably, for most women with ovarian cancer, this dance does not last long.

Three years after she went into remission, McLeod's cancer returned. Unfortunately, her experience is typical. The Harbin Clinic Cancer Center in Rome, Georgia, states, "Approximately 40–50 percent of the women who do achieve a remission after first-line chemotherapy will experience a recurrence of cancer within three years." McLeod again had surgery, and doctors removed three tumors. The surgery was followed by another six rounds of chemotherapy. Once again, she was pronounced cancer free. At this point she realized what scientists at Cancer Research UK already knew: "For most women with advanced ovarian cancer, or cancer that has come back after treatment, it is not possible to cure it."

Doctors refer to the treatment of recurrent cancer like McLeod's as salvage therapy, and the decision to use such therapy must be weighed against the risks. Physicians at Texas Oncology in Dallas note, "The purpose of receiving cancer treatment may be to improve symptoms through local control of the cancer, increase a patient's chance of cure, or prolong a patient's survival." In the case of recurrent ovarian cancer, salvage therapy is generally used for the latter reason. Nonetheless, a patient and her team of specialists must work together to determine if more surgery and chemotherapy are worth the risks. The biggest risk is the buildup of toxins in the patient's body, which can cause additional illnesses and even prevent the salvage therapy from working. In addition, over time the cancer can become resistant to chemotherapy drugs, which makes each new recurrence harder to treat.

Four years after her second battle with ovarian cancer, McLeod suffered another recurrence. More than a decade after her initial diagnosis, she found herself facing another course of salvage therapy. As the American Cancer Society notes in the "Survivorship: During and After Treatment" section of its website, "Your new 'normal' may include making changes in the way you eat, the things you do, and your sources of support. It will mean making treatment part of your everyday life—treatments that you may be getting for the rest of your life."

Instead of dwelling on her disease, McLeod has chosen to act. She is an advocate for women suffering from ovarian cancer, raising money for the cause and starting a support group for survivors. According to the Ovarian Cancer National Alliance, statistics compiled by the Centers for Disease Control and Prevention reveal that "the mortality rates for ovarian cancer have not improved in forty years since the 'War on Cancer' was declared." Given this stark truth, it is essential that women like McLeod continue fighting to bring attention to this deadly disease.

In *Perspectives on Diseases and Disorders: Ovarian Cancer*, the authors present a variety of viewpoints on how the disease can be detected, treated, and managed. In chapter 1, among other topics, the authors discuss methods of diagnosing the disease, alternative therapies, and the latest advances in treatment. In chapter 2 the authors debate issues such as whether fertility drugs cause ovarian cancer, whether early detection improves survival, and the role of oral contraception in preventing the disease. The final chapter focuses on the experiences of women with ovarian cancer.

CHAPTER 1

Understanding Ovarian Cancer

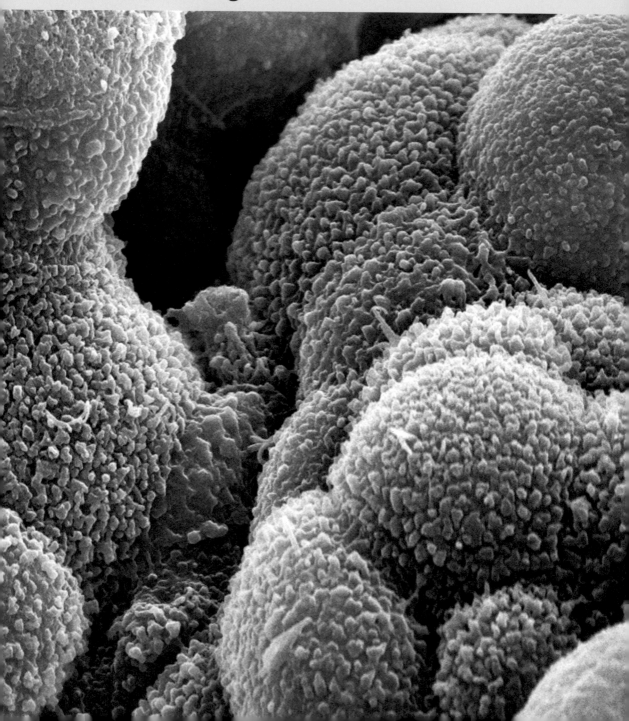

Ovarian Cancer: An Overview

Christopher Dolinsky and Carolyn Vachani

OncoLink is an online web service providing information about all forms of cancer. It is supported by the Abramson Cancer Center of the University of Pennsylvania. In the following viewpoint Christopher Dolinsky and Carolyn Vachani, researchers at the center, provide an overview of ovarian cancer. Although there are known risk factors for ovarian cancer, such as age and family history, there are no proven ways of preventing the disease. In addition, current screen tests, pelvic exams, and genetic screening are not yet capable of accurately predicting which women will develop the disease. Unfortunately, the authors note, the signs for ovarian cancer mimic other diseases and are easily missed; as a result, many women are not diagnosed until they are in the most severe stage of the disease. Current treatment options are limited and not guaranteed to be effective.

Photo on facing page. A colored electron micrograph shows cancerous epithelial cells of the ovary. Epithelian ovarian cancer accounts for 90 percent of all ovarian cancers. (© Steve Gschmeissner/Photo Researchers, Inc.)

Ovarian cancer develops when cells in the ovaries begin to grow in an uncontrolled fashion with the potential to invade nearby tissues or spread throughout the body. Large collections of this "out-of-control" tissue are often referred to as tumors. However, some tumors are not really cancer because they cannot spread or threaten someone's life. These are called benign tumors or masses. The tumors that can spread throughout the body or invade nearby tissues represent true invasive cancer, and are called malignant tumors. The distinction between benign and malignant tumors is very important in ovarian cancer because many ovarian tumors are benign. Also, sometimes women (especially young women) can get ovarian cysts, which are collections of fluid in the ovaries that can occasionally grow large or become painful. However, ovarian cysts are not cancerous and should not be confused with ovarian cancer. Your doctor may suggest that you have an ovarian cyst removed if it is becoming bothersome.

Cancers are characterized by the cells from which they originally form. The most common type of ovarian cancer is called epithelial ovarian cancer; it comes from cells that lie on the surface of the ovary known as epithelial cells. Epithelial ovarian cancer comprises about 90% of all ovarian cancers and usually occurs in older women. About 5% of ovarian cancers are called germ cell ovarian cancers and arise from the ovarian cells that produce eggs. Germ cell ovarian cancers are more likely to affect younger women. Another 5% of ovarian cancers are known as stromal ovarian cancers and develop from the cells in the ovary that hold the ovary together and produce hormones. These tumors can create symptoms by producing a large excess of female hormones. Each of these three types of ovarian cancer (epithelial, germ cell, stromal) contains many different subtypes of cancer that are distinguished based on how the cells look under a microscope. . . .

Risks and Prevention of Ovarian Cancer

As women get older, their risk of developing ovarian cancer increases. In the U.S., it was estimated that 21,990 women would develop ovarian cancer in 2011; and 15,460 women would die of ovarian cancer in 2011. Ovarian cancer accounts for 3% of all cancers in women, and is the 5th most common cause of cancer death for women in the U.S. Unfortunately, the majority of cases of ovarian cancer are found when it is advanced, because early stage ovarian cancers rarely cause any symptoms. It is for this reason that many researchers are interested in developing a screening test for ovarian cancer.

Although there are several known risk factors for getting ovarian cancer, no one knows exactly why one woman gets it and another does not. The most significant risk factor for developing ovarian cancer is age; the older a woman is, the higher her chances are of having it. The majority of ovarian cancers are diagnosed in women after they have gone through menopause, in their late fifties and sixties. The average age for a woman to get a sporadic ovarian cancer (meaning not part of a familial syndrome) is 63 years old, although women with genetic or familial risk factors tend to get ovarian cancer at a slightly younger age (average age of diagnosis is 54 years). Less than 15% of ovarian cancers are diagnosed in women under age 50. Many of these cases are not epithelial (the most common type) and are not amenable to screening with CA-125 [a protein often elevated in ovarian cancer].

Other than age, the next most important risk factor for ovarian cancer is a family history of ovarian cancer, particularly if your family members are affected at an early age. If your mother, sister, or daughters have had ovarian cancer, then you have an increased risk for development of the disease. Scientists estimate that 7% to 10% of all ovarian cancers are the result of hereditary genetic syndromes. . . .

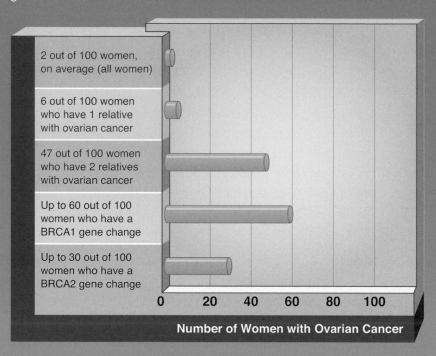

Number of Women Who Get Ovarian Cancer

Among risk factors for ovarian cancer, shown here, are changes in the genes BRCA1 and BRCA2.

2 out of 100 women, on average (all women)

6 out of 100 women who have 1 relative with ovarian cancer

47 out of 100 women who have 2 relatives with ovarian cancer

Up to 60 out of 100 women who have a BRCA1 gene change

Up to 30 out of 100 women who have a BRCA2 gene change

0   20   40   60   80   100

Number of Women with Ovarian Cancer

Taken from: National Ovarian Cancer Network, November 1, 2010, www.ovca.org/ovarian-cancer-causes.

The rest of the risk factors for ovarian cancer are not as significant as age and family history/genetic syndromes, but are mentioned because some of them can be controlled. It appears that the more menstrual cycles (and thus ovulations) a woman has in her lifetime, the more likely she is to develop ovarian cancer. Thus women who started menstruating early, go through menopause late, don't have any children (or have children after age 30), don't use a form of birth control that stops menstruation/ovulation (like birth control pills), and/or who don't breastfeed are all more likely to develop ovarian cancer. It also appears that having a tubal ligation (having your tubes tied) and/or a hysterectomy (having your uterus surgically removed) decreases your risk of ovarian cancer. Prolonged use of the infertility drug, clomiphene citrate, without getting pregnant can also slightly increase a woman's risk for ovarian cancer. Finally, it has been suggested that a diet high in animal fats can increase a woman's risk for ovarian cancer. Remember that all risk factors are based on probabilities, and even someone without any risk factors can still get ovarian cancer. Talk to your doctor about your risk factors for ovarian cancer to understand his/her recommendations for screening and prevention.

Unfortunately, there aren't very good screening methods for ovarian cancer, so preventing it is a particularly important challenge. If you are a woman without a family history/genetic syndrome, then the best way to prevent ovarian cancer is to alter whatever risk factors you have control over. For example, having children by age 30 and breastfeeding both reduce risk. Additionally, the use of oral contraceptives for 4 or more years is associated with an approximately 50% reduction in ovarian cancer risk in the general population. Bilateral tubal ligation and hysterectomy also decrease ovarian cancer risk. Keep in mind that any medication, including birth control pills, or surgical procedure, has its own risks and should not be taken lightly.

Screening Tests

The ideal screening test for ovarian cancer would save many lives. The vast majority of ovarian cancers are found at advanced stages, because early, small ovarian cancers are asymptomatic or have vague symptoms and cannot usually be found by a physician's exam. Patients who are diagnosed with early ovarian cancers tend to respond to treatment better than patients with more advanced cancers. Currently, there are not any effective approaches to ovarian cancer screening. There are a few tests that are being studied, but we need further data before they become routine for ovarian cancer screening.

Right now, the only screening that is recommended for the general population (women without hereditary cancer syndromes) is an annual pelvic examination. Your physician can usually feel your ovaries during the bi-manual portion of the exam, and if any abnormalities are felt, you can be referred for further tests. The major limitation to this method is that early ovarian cancers aren't usually appreciated on examination, and are often missed.

There are a few other tests that are currently being studied for ovarian cancer screening. One is a blood test that looks for a protein named CA-125. CA-125 is a protein that is shed from damaged ovary cells, and is often elevated in ovarian cancer. There are a few problems with CA-125 as a screening test. It is elevated in many other diseases and conditions besides ovarian cancer, including other cancers, endometriosis, fibroids, menstruation, colitis, diverticulitis, pancreatitis, lupus, and inflammation of the lining of the lung or heart. Only 50% of early stage ovarian cancers cause an elevated CA-125, and non-epithelial ovarian tumors do not produce CA-125. . . .

Another investigational method for ovarian cancer screening is transvaginal ultrasonography. Ultrasound is an imaging technique that uses sound waves that bounce off of tissues and provide a picture of whatever is being investigated. By inserting an ultrasound probe into a woman's vagina, doctors can get a relatively good look at her ovaries. If the ovaries look suspicious, then further tests can be done. The biggest problem with using transvaginal ultrasound for ovarian cancer screening is the same problem as using CA-125; both tests cause too many healthy women to require unnecessary procedures because the tests are not specific enough for ovarian cancer. Doctors hoped that a combination of CA-125 and transvaginal ultrasound would be an effective method

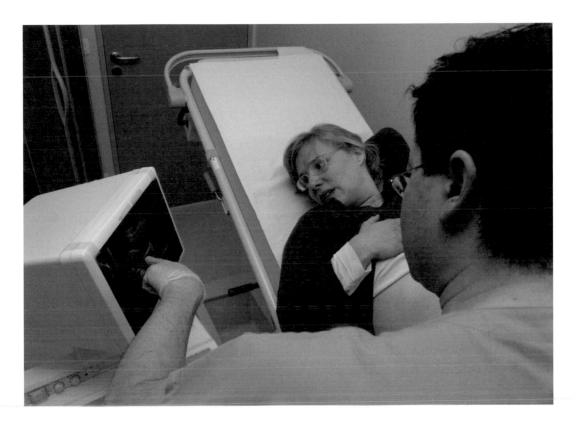

for ovarian cancer screening. However, results from a large study (United States National Institute of Health Prostate, Lung, Colorectal and Ovary Study) that combined both tests found that ovarian cancer mortality was not reduced by this screening approach. There is a second large, ongoing study of these tests called the UK Collaborative Trial of Ovarian Cancer Screening.

A urine screening test that identifies levels of a protein called Bcl-2 is in early clinical trials. Researchers have found that this protein was 10 times higher in women with ovarian cancer when compared to healthy individuals and those with benign ovarian disease. In early studies, the test detected 92% of ovarian cancers.

Currently, the general population should only be screened for ovarian cancer with a pelvic examination. However, women with a strong family history or those

A woman receives an ultrasound as part of a pelvic exam. Annual pelvic exams are important since, among other things, a physician can check for abnormalities in the ovaries that may signal cancerous tumors. (© **BSIP/Corbis**)

with a proven hereditary cancer syndrome may need to get more rigorous screening with serial CA-125 tests and/or transvaginal ultrasounds. Talk to your doctor about your ovarian cancer risk, and what the best way to go about screening is in your particular case.

What Are the Signs of Ovarian Cancer?

For many years, ovarian cancer has been called a "silent killer" because it was thought that symptoms did not develop until the disease was advanced. Recently, ovarian cancer experts found that this was not true, and most women had symptoms early on that were dismissed by themselves or their healthcare providers. Experts collaborated to develop the Ovarian Cancer Symptoms Consensus Statement, which describes important symptoms.

The symptoms that are more likely seen in women with ovarian cancer than healthy women include:

• Bloating
• Pelvic or abdominal pain
• Difficulty eating or feeling full quickly
• Urinary symptoms (urgency or frequency)

While these symptoms are more often due to other medical problems, women with ovarian cancer report that the symptoms persist and represent a change from their normal. The frequency and number of these symptoms are also key factors in the diagnosis.

Women who experience these symptoms almost daily for more than a few weeks should see a healthcare provider (preferably a gynecologist) for evaluation. . . .

Diagnosis and Staging of Ovarian Cancer

Ovarian cancer is a type of cancer that needs to be diagnosed and staged during a surgery. Often, the cancer is diagnosed and treated during the same procedure. Surgeries for ovarian cancer diagnosis and treatment should be done by a surgeon specialized in gynecologic malignancies. Surgery is done so that samples of the mass and surrounding tissue can be biopsied and analyzed. A biopsy is the only way to know for sure if you have cancer, because it allows your doctors to get cells that can be examined under a microscope. Once the tissue is removed, a doctor called a pathologist will review the specimen. The pathologist can tell if it is cancer or not; and if it is cancerous, the pathologist will characterize it by what type of tissue it arose from and what subtype of ovarian cancer it is, how abnormal it looks (called the grade), and whether or not it is invading surrounding tissues.

In order to guide treatment and offer some insight into prognosis, ovarian cancer is staged into four different groups at the time of the surgery. Surgeons who specialize in gynecologic malignancies go through a careful inspection and sampling of a woman's pelvis during this procedure, and biopsy specimens are sent to a pathologist for immediate examination while the surgeon is still working. The staging system used for ovarian cancer is called the FIGO system (International Federation of [Gynecology and Obstetrics]). The staging system is somewhat complex, but here is a simplified version of it:

Stage I: ovarian cancer confined to one or both ovaries. Cancer cells may also be present on the outside of the ovary or in the abdominal fluid.

Stage II: ovarian cancer that has spread beyond the ovaries, but is confined to the pelvis (can be in the uterus, bladder or rectum).

Stage III: ovarian cancer that has spread within the abdomen or pelvis, which may include the peritoneum (the lining of the abdomen), bowel, surface of the liver and/or lymph nodes

Stage IV: ovarian cancer that has distant spread (metastasis) to other organs

In addition to stage, the tumor grade will also be evaluated. This refers to how abnormal cells appear under a microscope. Low grade (or grade 1) tumors appear the most like normal cells, whereas higher grade tumors (grades 3 and 4) appear very abnormal under the microscope. Higher grade tumors may behave more aggressively than low grade tumors.

Generally, the higher the stage, the more serious the cancer. . . .

Treatments for Ovarian Cancer

Surgery. Almost all women with ovarian cancer will have some type of surgery in the course of their treatment. The purpose of surgery is first to diagnose and stage the cancer, and then to remove as much of the cancer as possible. In early stage cancers (stage I and II), surgeons can often remove all of the visible cancer. Generally, women with ovarian cancer will have a hysterectomy (removal of the uterus) and bilateral salpingo-oophorectomy (removal of both ovaries and fallopian tubes) as part of their operation. This is because there is always a risk of microscopic disease in both of the ovaries and the uterus. The only circumstance in which a woman may not have this entire operation is if she has a very early stage cancer (IA) that looks favorable under the microscope (grade 1). This is often the case with germ cell ovarian tumors. If a woman's tumor has these characteristics and she desires to maintain the ability to have children, then the surgeons can remove only her diseased ovary and tube. Then after she is done having children, she will need to have her uterus and the other tube and ovary removed. With any other stage or grade of tumor, or in patients finished with childbearing, the entire operation should be performed in order to provide the best possible chance for a cure.

Women who have more advanced disease (stage III or IV) will often have debulking surgeries, which means that their surgeon will attempt to remove as much disease as possible. Data collected in many studies has demonstrated that the more tumor that it debulked, the better the long term outcome for the patient. Sometimes ovarian cancer is diffusely spread throughout the entire pelvis and abdomen, and it can take a surgeon quite some time to get it adequately debulked. . . .

Another way that surgery is occasionally used in ovarian cancer is to closely monitor a patient for signs of recurrent disease. This is called a second look surgery, and can be done with an abdominal incision (a laparotomy) or using fiberoptic scopes and long, narrow tools which allow surgeons to operate less invasively (laparoscopically). This used to be a very common procedure, but studies failed to show a strong benefit from performing second look surgeries. Therefore, this procedure should only be done in the context of a clinical trial.

Chemotherapy. Despite the fact that the tumors are removed during surgery, there is always a risk of recurrence because there may be microscopic cancer cells left that the surgeon cannot remove. In order to decrease a patient's risk of recurrence, they are offered chemotherapy. Chemotherapy is the use of anti-cancer drugs that go throughout the entire body. The vast majority of patients with ovarian cancer should be offered chemotherapy after their surgery. The higher the stage of cancer you have, the more important it is that you receive chemotherapy. Generally, only very early stage cancers (early stage I) that look favorable under the microscope (grade 1 or 2) can be treated with surgery alone. Any woman with a more advanced stage or grade cancer should be offered chemotherapy.

There are many different chemotherapy drugs available, and treatments often combine several drugs to create a regimen. For the treatment of ovarian cancers, chemotherapy is typically given intravenously (into a vein) or directly into the abdomen (intraperitoneal [IP]) and is given in a clinic or hospital. With intraperitoneal chemotherapy, the chemotherapy is given directly into the abdomen

> **FAST FACT**
>
> According to *CA: A Cancer Journal for Clinicians,* in 2009, 21,550 new cases of ovarian cancer were diagnosed, and 14,600 women died of the disease.

through a catheter, allowed to "dwell" in the abdomen, coating the area in chemotherapy. After several hours, fluid is drained from the abdomen, releasing the chemotherapy remaining in the abdomen. Several large studies have shown significant survival advantages for women with good surgical debulking followed by intraperitoneal chemotherapy given with or without intravenous chemotherapy. Concerns over quality of life, technical difficulty of the procedure and lack of reimbursement for the procedure have limited the widespread use of IP therapy. . . .

Once a patient has been treated for ovarian cancer, they need to be closely followed for a recurrence.

Risk Factors for Ovarian Cancer

Christian Nordqvist

Christian Nordqvist is the cofounder and lead writer for MediLexicon International, a worldwide clearinghouse for medical information, and the author of more than eighty books, including *English for the Pharmaceutical Industry*. In the following viewpoint he argues that the exact cause of ovarian cancer is not known. Nonetheless, researchers have discovered many risk factors that increase the likelihood of developing the disease. According to Nordqvist, these factors include family history, age, reproductive issues, lifestyle, and overall health.

Although we know that ovarian cancer, like many other cancers, is caused by cells dividing and multiplying in an unordered way, nobody completely understands why cancer of the ovary occurs. We know that the following risk factors are linked to a higher chance of developing the disease:

Family History and Age

Most women who develop ovarian cancer do not have an inherited gene mutation. Women with close relatives who have/had ovarian cancer, as well as breast cancer, have a higher risk of developing ovarian cancer compared to other women. There are two genes—BRCA1 and BRCA2—which significantly raise the risk. The BRCA1 and BRCA2 genes also raise the risk of breast cancer. Those genes are inherited. The BRCA1 gene is estimated to increase ovarian cancer risk by 35% to 70%, and the BRCA2 by 10% to 30%. People of Ashkenazi Jewish descent are at particularly high risk of carrying these types of gene mutations.

Women with close relatives who have/had colon cancer, prostate cancer or uterine cancer are also at higher risk of ovarian cancer.

A researcher analyzes the DNA sequence of a cancer cell. Genetic screening can determine whether someone carries the genes BRCA1 and/ or BRCA2, which significantly raise the risk of contracting ovarian cancer.
(© Colin Cuthbert/Photo Researchers, Inc.)

Genetic screening can determine whether somebody carries the BRCA1 and/or BRCA2 genes. Although a test for gene mutations known to significantly increase the risk of hereditary breast or ovarian cancer has been available for more than a decade, a study by researchers from Massachusetts General Hospital found that few women with family histories of these cancers are even discussing genetic testing with their physicians or other health care providers.

After eight years of searching, an international team of scientists found a single nucleotide polymorphism (SNP) on chromosome 9 that is uniquely linked to ovarian cancer. The scientists estimated that women carrying that particular version of the SNP on both copies of chromosome 9 have a 40 per cent higher lifetime risk of developing ovarian cancer than women who do not carry it on either copy of chromosome 9, while women with only one copy of the variant have a 20 per cent higher lifetime risk of developing ovarian cancer than women who have none.

The majority of ovarian cancers occur in women over 65 years of age. A higher percentage of post-menopausal women develop ovarian cancer compared to pre-menopausal women.

Reproductive Issues

There is a link between the total number of ovulations during a woman's life and the risk of ovarian cancer. Four principal factors influence the total:

- Never having been pregnant—women who have never become pregnant have a higher risk of developing ovarian cancer compared to women who have become pregnant. The more times a woman has become pregnant the lower her risk is.
- Never having taken the contraceptive pill—women who have never been on the contraceptive pill have

a higher risk of developing ovarian cancer compared to women who have. Taking the Pill for 15 years halves the risk of ovarian cancer, a study by the Collaborative Group on Epidemiological Studies of Ovarian Cancer found.

• Early start of menstruation (early menarche)— women who started their periods at an early age have a higher risk of developing ovarian cancer.

• Late start of menopause—women whose menopause started at a later age than average have a higher risk of developing ovarian cancer.

Scientists at the Centers for Disease Control and Prevention (CDC) found that survival among women with ovarian cancer is also influenced by age of menarche (when periods start) and total number of lifetime ovulatory cycles.

Women who have had their fallopian tubes tied (tubal ligation) are estimated to have a 67% lower risk of ovarian cancer. A hysterectomy is said to reduce the risk by about one third.

Some studies have found a link between infertility treatment and a higher risk of ovarian cancer. Nobody is yet sure whether the risk is linked to infertility treatment, just infertility itself, or both. A Danish study published in the peer-reviewed *British Medical Journal* concluded that the use of fertility drugs does not increase a woman's risk of developing ovarian cancer. The study involved 54,362 women with infertility problems referred to all Danish fertility clinics between 1963 and 1998.

Women who have been diagnosed with breast cancer have a higher risk of developing ovarian cancer.

HRT [hormone replacement therapy] slightly increases a women's risk of developing ovarian cancer. Experts say the risk grows the longer the HRT continues,

FAST FACT

According to a 1993 study published in the journal *Cancer,* women under the age of thirty are very unlikely to develop cancer.

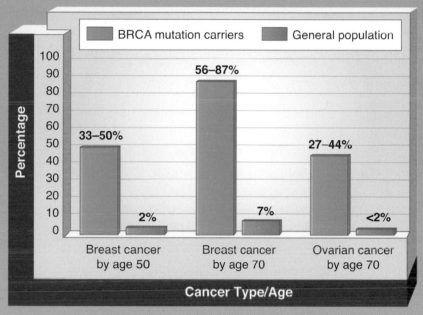

Mutation of BRCA Genes Increases the Risk of Cancer

Legend: BRCA mutation carriers / General population

Percentage (y-axis): 0, 10, 20, 30, 40, 50, 60, 70, 80, 90, 100

- Breast cancer by age 50: 33–50% (BRCA mutation carriers), 2% (general population)
- Breast cancer by age 70: 56–87% (BRCA mutation carriers), 7% (general population)
- Ovarian cancer by age 70: 27–44% (BRCA mutation carriers), <2% (general population)

Cancer Type/Age (x-axis)

Taken from: Abraham Shashoua. "BRCA 1/2 Testing." Breast and Ovarian Cancer Syndrome: Testing and Management. http://breastovariancancergene.com/breast_ovarian_cancer_test.html.

and returns to normal as soon as treatment stops. Danish scientists reported that compared with women who have never taken hormone therapy, those who currently take it or who have taken it in the past are at increased risk of ovarian cancer, regardless of the duration of use.

A UK study that was published in the peer-reviewed medical journal *The Lancet* suggested that between 1991 and 2005, an extra 1,000 women in the UK died of ovarian cancer because they were on Hormone Replacement Therapy.

Lifestyle and Overall Health

A study in the Netherlands found a link between acrylamide, a carcinogenic compound found in cooked, and especially burned, carbohydrate rich foods, and increased risk of endometrial and ovarian cancer in postmenopausal women.

Being obese or overweight increases the risk of developing many cancers. The more overweight you are, the higher the risk. Several studies have also shown that obese cancer patients are more likely to have faster advancing ones compared to cancer patients of normal weight. Obese older women who have never used hormone replacement therapy have nearly twice the risk of their normal weight peers of developing ovarian cancer, according to a study by the researchers at the National Cancer Institute.

Women who develop endometriosis have an approximately 30% higher risk of developing ovarian cancer compared to other women. Endometriosis is a condition in which cells that are normally found inside the uterus (endometrial cells) are found growing outside of the uterus. Danazol, a medication used to treat endometriosis, has been linked to ovarian cancer risk.

Types and Stages of Ovarian Cancer

Jeffrey L. Stern

Jeffrey L. Stern is a clinical professor of gynecologic oncology at the University of California–San Francisco and the director of gynecologic oncology at the Women's Cancer Center of Northern California at the Alta Bates Summit Comprehensive Cancer Center. In the following viewpoint he notes that ovarian cancer comes in different forms, which are distinguished by the way they infect the body. The prognosis for ovarian cancer sufferers can be determined by the stage of the disease. There are four stages, with the fourth stage being the most severe and least survivable. Treatment type and duration, Stern explains, depend largely upon the stage of the disease.

Carcinoma of the ovary is one of the most common gynecologic malignancies. In many cases, it is curable when found early, but because it does not cause any symptoms in its early stages, most women have widespread disease at the time of diagnosis. Partly because of this, the mortality rate from ovarian cancer exceeds that for all other gynecologic malignancies combined. It is the fourth most frequent cause of death in women in the United States. About one in every 70 women will develop cancer of the ovary and one in every 100 women will die from it. The American Cancer Society estimates that there will be 26,000 cases of ovarian cancer diagnosed each year with approximately 15,000 deaths.

Types of Ovarian Cancer

The most common form of ovarian cancer arises from the cells covering the surface of the ovary and is known as epithelial carcinoma. There are five major types of this carcinoma—serous, mucinous, endometrioid, clear cell and undifferentiated. Epithelial carcinomas are further divided into grades, according to how virulent they appear on microscopic examination.

Tumors of low malignant potential, also known as borderline tumors, are the most well-differentiated malignancy (Grade 0) and account for 15 percent of all epithelial carcinomas of the ovary. The other three grades are well-differentiated (Grade 1), moderately-differentiated (Grade 2) and poorly-differentiated (Grade 3). Well-differentiated tumors have a better prognosis than poorly-differentiated tumors. Clear cell carcinoma and especially undifferentiated carcinoma have a poorer prognosis than the other cell types.

The two other major kinds of ovarian cancer—germ cell tumors, which arise from the eggs, and ovarian stromal tumors, which arise from supportive tissue—are relatively uncommon and account for less than 10 percent of all ovarian malignancies.

How It Spreads

Ovarian cancer spreads early by shedding malignant cells into the abdominal cavity. The cells implant on the lining of the abdominal cavity (peritoneum) and can grow

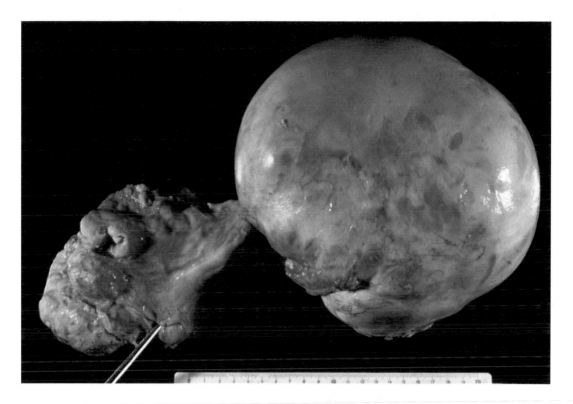

on the surface of the liver, the fatty tissue attached to the stomach and large intestine (omentum), the small and large intestines, the bladder and the diaphragm.

Disease on the diaphragm may at times result in impaired drainage of fluid from the abdominal cavity, resulting, for some women, in a large collection of abdominal fluid known as ascites. The cancer cells spread to the surface of the lungs and chest cavity, resulting in a collection of fluid around the lungs known as a pleural effusion.

Ovarian cancer may also spread to the pelvic, aortic, groin and neck lymph nodes. . . .

Shown here is a specimen of an epithelial carcinoma of the ovary. The cancer arises from the ovary's surface tissues and invades the supporting tissue of the ovaries, often spreading to other parts of the body. (© CNRI/Photo Researchers, Inc.)

Risk Factors

There is a much higher incidence of ovarian cancer in industrialized countries. Some researchers have implicated talcum powder, which until recently contained asbestos, as a possible cause. Ovarian cancer can occur in any age group, but is most common in postmenopausal women. Not ovulating—by having children, breastfeeding, using birth control pills or having a condition that interferes with ovulation such as polycystic ovaries—has been shown to offer protection against developing cancer. There may also be a genetic predisposition to this cancer. There are rare families in which several members of the same or different generation develop ovarian cancer. This is known as hereditary ovarian cancer syndrome. Women with hereditary ovarian cancer syndrome are also at significant risk for the development of breast cancer, uterine cancer, and colon cancer. These individuals are often positive for the BRCA-1 or BRCA-2 gene, which can be tested for. It generally affects women in their mid-forties. There may be up to a 50 percent risk of developing ovarian cancer in their lifetime. It can also be inherited through the male side of the family. This syndrome occurs in less than 3 percent of all women who have a positive family history of ovarian cancer. Approximately 7 percent of all women with ovarian cancer do not seem to have a genetic disposition but have a positive family history. Ninety percent of these women have only one other family member with ovarian cancer.

> **FAST FACT**
>
> According to the Ovarian Cancer Research Fund, the majority of ovarian cancers, approximately 85 to 90 percent, begin in the epithelium, a tissue that covers the surface of the ovary.

Suggested management in women with a family history for ovarian cancer is as follows: Removal of both ovaries and sometimes the uterus after childbearing or very close follow-up with serum CA-125 and pelvic ultrasound for those women who have hereditary ovarian cancer syndrome. If there is a family history of only one relative with ovarian cancer, prophylactic removal of the ovaries is not recommended. In women who are BRCA-1 or BRCA-2 negative and who have 2–3 close relatives with ovarian cancer, prophylactic removal of the ovaries is generally recommended by most gyn [gynecologic] oncologists and geneticists.

Screening

There are no diagnostic methods accurate enough to be used for routine screening of women without symptoms. Nonetheless, it is recommended that all women have an annual pelvic and rectal examination since an ovarian mass can occasionally be detected. A Pap smear will detect ovarian cancer in only 10 percent of women with the disease. Studies have shown that a serum tumor marker known as CA-125 is elevated in 90 percent of women with advanced epithelial ovarian cancer and only 50% of women with cancer confined to the ovary (Stage I). Unfortunately, this test is not accurate enough for screening all women for ovarian cancer. Approximately 2 percent of normal women will have an elevated CA-125 (normal is less than 35). Approximately 1 percent of normal women will have a CA-125 greater than 65. Because of the small incidence of false-positive tests, screening all women with CA-125 has not been recommended. A great deal of research is taking place exploring the use of CA-125 as well as other tumor markers for screening. Tumor markers are, however, useful for assessing response to therapy.

A pelvic ultrasound (sonogram) examination may become a part of the routine annual gynecologic examination in the future. It is performed using a minimally uncomfortable vaginal probe, as well as through the abdominal wall. It is used to examine the ovaries as well as the uterus. When used in combination with CA-125, it is fairly accurate in detecting ovarian neoplasms [tumors].

A small number of women have hereditary ovarian cancer syndrome and have a gene in their chromosomes, known as the BRCA-1 or BRCA-2 gene. It may be possible to test women who are thought to be carriers for this gene. If so, counseling or therapeutic intervention can be instituted (see risk factors).

Common Signs and Symptoms

Many women with early stages of ovarian carcinoma have no symptoms. The unfortunate result is that two-thirds of all women with ovarian carcinoma have advanced disease at the time of diagnosis.

Many women have vague, non-specific abdominal symptoms including pain, pelvic pressure, low back discomfort, mild nausea, feeling full early when eating, constipation and gas. Some women have abnormal uterine bleeding. Although some cases are diagnosed during a routine gynecologic examination, many women are diagnosed only when they have developed abdominal distention because of ascites.

Advanced ovarian cancer often results in blockage of the intestines, causing severe nausea, vomiting, pain and weight loss.

Diagnosis

Physical examination:

- A careful pelvic exam is performed with attention to the ovaries, uterus, bladder and rectum.
- The neck, groin and underarms (axillae) are examined for enlarged lymph nodes.
- The lungs are carefully examined for excess fluid.
- The abdomen is examined for the presence of an enlarged liver, a mass or ascites.

Blood and other tests:

- Complete blood count (CBC).
- Serum liver and kidney function tests.
- Serum CA-125.

Imaging:

- Abdominal and pelvic CT [computed tomography] or MRI [magnetic resonance imaging] scans may be obtained in advanced cases.
- X-rays of the upper gastrointestinal tract (UGI series) may occasionally be done.

- Intravenous pyelogram [an X-ray procedure done to test kidney function] (occasionally).
- Barium enema (occasionally).

Endoscopy and biopsy:

A diagnosis requires microscopic examination of part or all of the involved ovary or any other suspicious abdominal mass. Cystic ovarian tumors that are less than 2-½ in. (6 cm) in diameter occurring in premenopausal women are usually benign cysts.

Surgical evaluation should be strongly considered for any ovarian mass in a postmenopausal woman, masses that are larger than 2-½ in. (6 cm) in diameter, masses persisting longer than one menstrual cycle and masses that are suspicious on imaging of the pelvis.

The Stages of Ovarian Cancer

Ovarian carcinoma is staged at surgery. Stages are usually defined according to the classification system devised by FIGO (International Federation of Gynecology and Obstetrics). The TNM system [based on the presence of Tumors, lymph Node involvement, and Metastases] corresponds to the stages accepted by FIGO.

Stage I:

Cancer confined to one or both ovaries.

- Ia: Cancer is limited to one ovary. There is no ascites and no tumor on the surface of the ovary and the surface of the tumor is unruptured.
- Ib: The cancer is limited to both ovaries. There is no ascites and no tumor on the surface of either ovary and the surfaces of the tumors are unruptured.
- Ic: The cancer is either Stage Ia or Ib and one or more of the following applies: there is tumor on the surface of one or both ovaries, at least one of the tumors has ruptured, ascites is present or the abdominal washings contain malignant cells.

Five-year survival [rate is] 60 to 100 percent, depending on the histologic [tissue] type, grade, and sub-stage.

Staging and Prognosis of Ovarian Cancer

Stage	Description	Frequency	5-year Survival
I	Cancer confined to the ovary or ovaries	23%	90%
II	Cancer confined to the true pelvis	13%	70%
III	Cancer spread into but confined to the abdomen	47%	15–20%
IV	Cancer spread outside the pelvis and abdomen	16%	1–5%

Taken from: Robert C. Young, "Gynecologic Malignancies," in *Harrison's Principles of Internal Medicine*, Dennis L. Kasper et al. eds. New York: McGraw-Hill, 2005.

Stage II:

The tumor involves one or both ovaries with extension to other pelvic structures.

- IIa: There is extension of the cancer or metastases to the uterus and/or fallopian tubes.
- IIb: There is extension to the bladder or rectum.
- IIc: The cancer is either stage IIa or IIb and one or more of the following applies: there is tumor on the surface of one or both ovaries, at least one of the tumors has ruptured, the ascites contains malignant cells or the washings from the abdominal cavity contain malignant cells.

Five-year survival [rate is] about 60–80 percent.

Stage III:

The tumor involves one or both ovaries with tumor implants confined to the abdominal cavity but outside the pelvis, or there is cancer in the pelvic, para-aortic or groin nodes.

- IIIa: The tumor is grossly limited to the pelvis and the lymph nodes are negative but there is biopsy-proven microscopic cancer on the intra-abdominal (peritoneal) surfaces.
- IIIb: The tumor involves one or both ovaries and there are tumor implants on the peritoneal surfaces less than ¾ in. (2 cm) in diameter. The lymph nodes are negative.
- IIIc: The tumor involves one or both ovaries, there are tumor implants on the surface of the abdominal cavity greater than ¾ in. (2 cm) in diameter or there is cancer in the pelvic, para-aortic or groin lymph nodes.

Five-year survival [rate is] about 20–50 percent.

Stage IV:
Growth involves one or both ovaries. There are distant metastases to the liver or lungs, or there are malignant cells in the excess fluid accumulated around the lungs.

Five-year survival [rate is] 10–25 percent.

Ovarian Cancer Treatment, Side Effects, and Follow-Up Care

Ovarian Cancer National Alliance

In the following viewpoint the Ovarian Cancer National Alliance (OCNA), an organization formed in 1977 to educate health care professionals and the public about ovarian cancer, states that there are four main treatment options: surgery, chemotherapy, intraperitoneal chemotherapy, and radiation therapy. The treatment type is chosen based on the kind and stage of the disease. According to the OCNA, the side effects of each treatment type can range from mild to severe and may even be permanent, as is sometimes the case if there is nerve damage. Follow-up care is essential for the long-term well-being of the patient.

Navigating and understanding treatment options are critical for an ovarian cancer patient's survival. All treatment decisions should be made by a patient in consultation with her medical professional.

Treatment Options

Surgery: During surgery, doctors attempt to remove all visible tumors (tumor debulking). The five-year survival rate and disease-free intervals of patients whose surgeon was a gynecologic oncologist far surpass those of patients whose surgeons were not oncologists.

Chemotherapy: Patients undergo chemotherapy in an effort to kill any cancer cells that remain in the body after surgery.

Intraperitoneal chemotherapy: This therapy places the medicine directly into the peritoneal area [the area around the groin and abdomen] through a surgically implanted port and catheter. While intraperitoneal (IP) therapy has been in use since the 1950s, new advances have combined it with intravenous (IV) therapy, using chemotherapy agents that work best for treating ovarian cancer. The National Cancer Institute recommends that, for select ovarian cancer patients, chemotherapy be given by both IV and IP. This combination has been found to increase survival for women with advanced stage ovarian cancer.

Neoadjuvant chemotherapy: Some patients may receive chemotherapy before having surgery to remove their tumors. This is known as neoadjuvant chemotherapy.

Other drugs: Other drugs, including angiogenesis inhibitors [which deter the growth of new blood vessels in tumors] and targeted therapies, may be recommended either in conjunction with chemotherapy or as single agents. These drugs may have very different side-effects than chemotherapies and may be useful only for specific populations.

Radiation therapy or radiotherapeutic procedures: These procedures may be used to kill cancer cells that remain in the pelvic area.

Clinical trials: Researchers carry out ovarian cancer clinical trials to find ways of improving medical care and

Intraperitoneal Chemotherapy

With intraperitoneal chemotherapy, the drugs attack cancer cells in the abdomen in a higher concentration than if they were administered through the bloodstream using intravenous therapy.

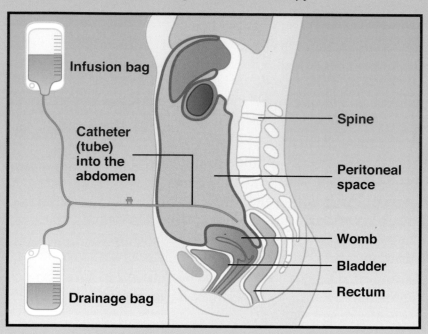

Infusion bag

Catheter (tube) into the abdomen

Drainage bag

Spine

Peritoneal space

Womb

Bladder

Rectum

Taken from: Cancer Research, UK, "Ovarian Cancer Research," http://cancerhelp.cancerresearchuk.org/type/ovarian-cancer/treatment/whats-new-in-ovarian-cancer-research.

treatment for women with this disease. A woman is eligible to participate in a clinical trial at any point in her experience with ovarian cancer: before, during or after treatment. Many women think of clinical trials as an option only after other treatments have failed. Clinical trials exist for women in this situation, but many equally important trials are available for women earlier in their fight against ovarian cancer.

Side Effects

The goal of chemotherapy is to eliminate rapidly growing cancerous cells; however, some drugs are unable to differentiate between cancerous cells and other frequently dividing cells. As a result, the drugs can kill cells found in the bone marrow, digestive tract, hair follicles, and reproductive organs. Every woman experiences different side effects depending on the type and dosage of her chemotherapy treatments. Women undergoing treatment should talk to their medical professionals about the best way to address their side effects.

Hair loss: Some chemotherapy drugs damage hair follicles, causing loss of body hair. Hair loss typically begins two to three weeks after the first treatment and may affect not only the hair on a woman's head but also her eyebrows, eyelashes, facial hair, pubic hair, underarm hair and leg hair. While hair loss can be extensive, it is almost always temporary. Women's hair usually grows back once treatment ends. Some women cope with hair loss by cutting their hair or shopping for a wig before losing any hair.

Nausea and vomiting: Since nausea is such a common side effect of chemotherapy, doctors will often prescribe antiemetics to minimize suffering. Antiemetics work by blocking signals between the brain and stomach to stop vomiting. These side effects must be managed during chemotherapy treatments because uncontrolled vomiting and nausea can interfere with the patient's ability to receive treatments. Complementary therapies, such as ginger, exist and are proven to reduce nausea.

Fatigue: Cancer patients experience fatigue for many reasons—not all of which are known. Both cancer and cancer treatments can cause fatigue. Fatigue is a common side effect following radiation and chemotherapy. Medication used to treat pain, depression, vomiting, seizures, and other side effects may cause fatigue. Fatigue usually lessens after treatment ceases, but sometimes people never regain their full energy.

Diarrhea and constipation: Diarrhea is a common side effect of chemotherapy that usually occurs in the days immediately following a chemotherapy treatment. Patients with diarrhea need to remember that they can become dehydrated quickly and should be sure to hydrate themselves. Some patients may experience constipation due to chemotherapy, the after effects of surgery, or anti-nausea drugs. Doctors often tell patients who experience constipation to take a mild laxative or stool softener. Patients experiencing constipation should drink plenty of liquids.

Nerve problems: Certain chemotherapy drugs can cause peripheral neuropathy, an increase in numbness caused by damage to the nerves that transmit signals between extremities and the central nervous system. This damage to the nerves often causes a tingling sensation or loss of control in the hands or feet. Acupuncture or massage and physical therapy may lessen these side effects, which are usually temporary and improve or resolve when chemotherapy treatment stops.

Mouth issues: Chemotherapy can kill the cells lining the mouth, throat, and gastrointestinal tract, causing mouth sores. Mouth issues are particularly bad for patients who receive high doses of chemotherapy, have poor oral and dental health prior to treatment, or have kidney or concomitant disease. Smoking, using tobacco, and consuming harsh foods or alcohol increase the severity of these side effects. Some chemotherapy drugs create taste changes in patients. Food may taste salty or bitter but usually tastes normal again once treatment is over. Non-alcoholic mouthwash and other products can decrease dryness of the mouth.

Sexuality and intimacy issues: Interest in sexual intimacy often decreases for chemotherapy patients for many reasons, including additional stress and the side effects of treatment. Patients need to maintain a positive self image during this time and sustain open commu-

FAST FACT

A 2011 report by the Stanford University Cancer Institute concludes that cancer patients can suffer from side effects of chemotherapy for months—and even years—after treatment.

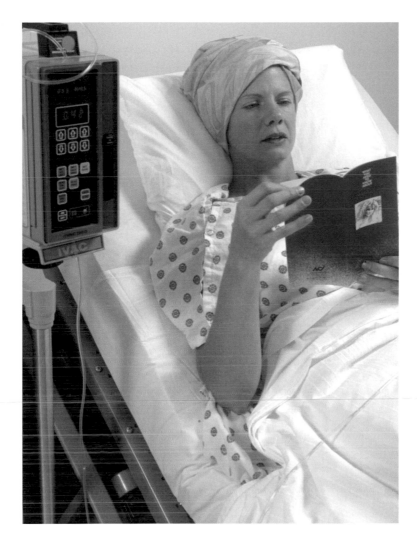

An ovarian cancer patient undergoes post-surgery chemotherapy treatment. The treatment typically results in a number of serious side effects. (© **Will & Deni McIntyre/ Photo Researchers, Inc.**)

nication with their partners. When a patient is ready to engage in sexual activity, she should consider taking the following actions:

- Make time for rest before and after sexual activity to preserve energy.
- Use water-soluble lubricants as her vagina may be drier than usual due to hormonal changes.
- Experiment to find comfortable positions and avoid those that will tire her quickly.

"Chemobrain": Many women experience forgetfulness and have trouble with concentration after receiving chemotherapy. This absentmindedness is often temporary; however, about 15 percent of chemo patients experience permanent problems. Since the cause is unknown, no treatment exists for this side effect. Women who have experienced this side effect offer several suggestions for dealing with it:

- Minimize distractions while performing important tasks.
- Keep a daily organizer/journal to keep track of appointments.
- Use the calendar on your computer and voicemail messages to remind yourself of meetings.

Follow-Up Plan After Treatment

After the initial treatment is over, a woman should have follow-up treatments with her doctor. During follow-ups, doctors do thorough physical exams and may also monitor a patient's blood for an elevated CA-125 level. Some patients have a sensitive CA-125 that will rise before their CT [computed tomography] scan shows evidence of recurrent disease; a recent study suggests that it may be more useful to wait until a woman experiences symptoms of ovarian cancer before starting treatment. Others will have evidence of the disease before their CA-125 rises. Doctors often use a combination of tests to monitor a patient because recurrent ovarian cancer has a wide spectrum of behavior making it difficult to monitor. In addition to physical exams and a CA-125 test, doctors may request CT and/or PET [positron emission tomography] scans to look for tumor growth.

A patient should discuss a follow-up plan and survivorship plan with her physician, clearly outlining a plan of action post treatment. A survivorship plan that addresses long-term issues is critical for a woman to have and discuss with her regular internist and other health care professionals outside of her cancer treatment.

CA-125 plus HE4 [human epididymis protein, a marker for ovarian cancer] have been approved by the Food and Drug Administration (FDA) for monitoring.

Recurrence

When cancer returns after a period of remission, it is considered a recurrence. A cancer recurrence happens because some cancer cells were left behind and eventually grow and become apparent. The cancer may come back to the same place as the original tumor or to another place in the body. Around 70 percent of patients diagnosed with ovarian cancer will have a recurrence.

One of the factors in determining a patient's risk of recurrence is the stage of the cancer at diagnosis:

- Patients diagnosed in stage I have a 10 percent chance of recurrence.
- Patients diagnosed in stage II have a 30 percent chance of recurrence.
- Patients diagnosed in stage III have a 70 to 90 percent chance of recurrence.
- Patients diagnosed in stage IV have a 90 to 95 percent chance of recurrence.

Recurrent ovarian cancer is treatable but rarely curable. Women with recurrent ovarian cancer may have to undergo another surgery. Because many women with recurrent ovarian cancer receive chemotherapy for a prolonged period of time, sometimes continuously, the toxicities of therapy are a major factor in treatment decisions.

The effectiveness and type of treatment for recurrent ovarian cancer depends on what kind of chemotherapy the patient received in the past, the side effects associated with previous treatments, the length of time since finishing the previous treatment, and the extent of the recurrent cancer. Chemotherapy is used to stop the progression of cancer and prolong the patient's survival. Sometimes, surgery is used to relieve symptoms, such as a blocked bowel caused by the recurrence.

A woman, in consultation with her doctor, should set realistic goals for what to expect from treatment. This may mean weighing the possible positive outcomes of a new treatment against the possible negative ones. At some point, a woman may decide that continuing treatment is unlikely to improve her health or survival. A woman must be certain that she is comfortable with her decision, whatever it is.

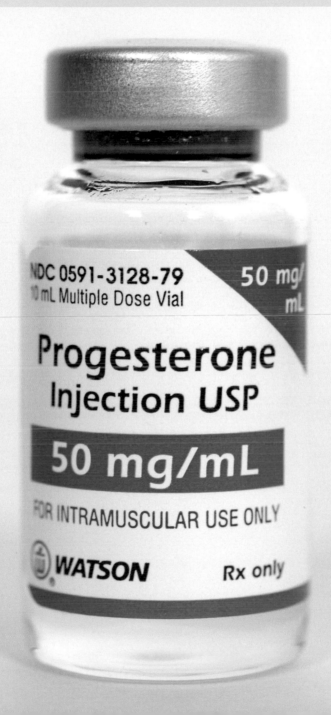

Fertility Drugs Do Not Cause Ovarian Cancer

Penelope M. Webb

Previous studies have indicated that prolonged use of common fertility medications increases the risk for developing ovarian cancer. In the following viewpoint Penelope M. Webb reports on a Danish study that argues that no such link can be established. The study, published in the *British Medical Journal* (*BMJ*), is the largest of its kind and included more than 54,000 women overall, among them 156 women with ovarian cancer. The study's author, Allan Jensen, and his colleagues compared data from infertile women who used fertility drugs and infertile women who did not. They found that there was no increased risk of ovarian cancer for those taking fertility medications. Future studies are needed to be certain that as the participants age and the risk for ovarian cancer climbs, the data remain relevant. Webb is a senior research fellow at *BMJ*.

Photo on previous page. Since the 1980s, a debate has persisted about whether the use of fertility drugs, such as progesterone, increase a woman's risk of developing ovarian cancer. (© John Kaprielian/Photo Researchers, Inc.)

SOURCE: Penelope M. Webb, "Fertility Drugs and Ovarian Cancer: Current Evidence Shows No Increased Risk," *British Medical Journal,* vol. 338, no. 3075, 2009. Copyright © 2009 by the British Medical Journal. All rights reserved. Reproduced by permission.

During the past two decades, considerable debate has [centered] around whether the use of fertility drugs increases a woman's risk of developing ovarian cancer. Most ovarian cancers are assumed to arise from the layer of epithelial cells surrounding the ovary, and it has been suggested that the repeated cycle of damage and repair that occurs with ovulation may lead to DNA damage and potentially cancer—the so called "incessant ovulation" hypothesis. By stimulating hyperovulation, fertility drugs might therefore increase the risk of cancer. A second hypothesis posits that increasing exposure to gonadotrophins increases the risk of ovarian cancer, and because gonadotrophins are used to treat infertility, such treatment might, theoretically, put patients at risk. In [his] study, [Allan] Jensen and colleagues use data from a large cohort study of infertile women to assess the effects of fertility drugs on the risk of ovarian cancer.

A woman demonstrates the use of a hormone injection pen. A study by researcher Allan Jensen found that increasing exposure to gonadotropin hormones—which are used to treat infertility—does not increase the risk of ovarian cancer.
(© **Medic Image/Universal Images Group/Getty Images**)

Previous Studies

Anxiety was initially fuelled by two studies suggesting that women who had taken fertility drugs had an increased risk of developing ovarian cancer. However, these studies included only 20 and 11 women with ovarian cancer who had used fertility drugs. Subsequent studies have generally reported no association, but concerns remain, particularly for women who undergo 12 or more cycles of treatment or who never succeed in becoming pregnant. For example, a Cochrane review on the use of clomifene citrate for unexplained subfertility mentions that use for more than 12 cycles has been associated with increased risk of ovarian cancer. Cochrane reviews are, rightly, highly respected and widely accessible to clinicians and patients, yet the body of the review suggests the statement about ovarian cancer risk is based solely on the results of the early studies. So should women seeking treatment for infertility be worried that fertility drugs might increase their risk of ovarian cancer?

More than 10 cohort studies and a similar number of case-control studies have attempted to answer this question. Most have been limited by small sample sizes—only three studies have included more than 25 women with ovarian cancer who have used fertility drugs. Furthermore, infertility itself is a risk factor for ovarian cancer, but many studies have been unable to separate the potential effects of the use of fertility drugs on the risk of ovarian cancer from the effects of the underlying infertility; others could not control for potentially important confounding factors such as parity [number of births] and use of oral contraceptives.

Jensen and colleagues' study included 54,362 women with infertility problems referred to Danish fertility clinics from 1963 to 1998. It found that use of four groups of

> **FAST FACT**
>
> The February 2002 issue of the *American Journal of Epidemiology* reports that while ovarian cancer is not caused by fertility medications, it can be linked to specific causes of infertility.

fertility drugs (gonadotrophins, clomifenes, human chorionic gonadotrophin, and gonadotrophin releasing hormone) was not associated with an overall increase in the risk of ovarian cancer. They also found no suggestion that risk was increased in women who had undergone 10 or more cycles of treatment or in those who remained nulliparous [childless]. Although the authors did see a significantly increased risk of the most common serous subtype of ovarian cancer in women who had used clomifene, this was just one of 20 separate comparisons in their subgroup analyses and was probably a chance association.

Study Importance

This study is important because it included 156 women with ovarian cancer, more than three times as many as any previous cohort study, and it compared infertile

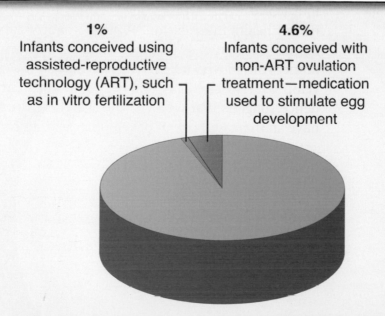

The Impact of Fertility Drugs on US Births

1%
Infants conceived using assisted-reproductive technology (ART), such as in vitro fertilization

4.6%
Infants conceived with non-ART ovulation treatment—medication used to stimulate egg development

Taken from: Centers for Disease Control and Prevention, "Fertility Drugs' Impact on US Births," February 24, 2010. www.cdc.gov/features/dsfertilitydrugs.

women who had used fertility drugs with infertile women who had not used fertility drugs. Although information on parity and use of oral contraceptives was unavailable for many women, analyses in the subgroup of women with this information suggested that adjusting for these variables would have had little effect on the results. However, although the study was much larger than previous investigations, it still could not exclude the possibility of a small increase in the risk of ovarian cancer in users of fertility drugs—the rate ratio for use of any fertility drug was 1.03, but the upper bound of the 95% confidence interval was 1.47. Larger numbers of women will need to be studied to answer this question, and these will come with further follow-up of the cohort as they enter the age range where ovarian cancer is most common.

These data are reassuring and provide further evidence that fertility drugs do not increase a woman's risk of ovarian cancer to any great extent, although small increases in risk cannot be ruled out. Given the increasing numbers of women seeking fertility treatment, this is important information for clinicians and their patients, and in a world where women increasingly turn to the internet for health information, clinicians should take time to discuss this matter so that women are properly informed. Some women who take fertility drugs will inevitably develop ovarian cancer by chance alone, but current evidence suggests that women who use these drugs do not have an increased risk of developing ovarian cancer.

Symptoms of Ovarian Cancer May Help with Early Detection

Nicole Fawcett

Previously, researchers have argued that no real symptoms existed for ovarian cancer. In the following viewpoint, however, Nicole Fawcett, news editor for the University of Michigan Comprehensive Cancer Center, argues that, according to recent research, ovarian cancer does reveal symptoms. Given that the majority of ovarian cancers go undetected until they are in advanced stages, Fawcett urges women to heed symptoms that could point to ovarian cancer, including abdominal bloating and pain, difficulty eating, and urinary problems. Based on this recent discovery, Fawcett recommends that women pay close attention to changes in their health and undergo a yearly pelvic exam.

O varian cancer doesn't get the kind of attention breast cancer gets. It's not as common, and because survival rates are poor, it does not produce an army of survivors to raise awareness. It's traditionally known as the "silent killer" because it was thought to reveal no symptoms in its earliest, most curable stages.

But ovarian cancer is silent no more. First, researchers recently reported a cluster of symptoms that can indicate ovarian cancer. And advocates—both survivors and families—are beginning to make noise and encourage awareness for this disease.

September is Ovarian Cancer Awareness Month and on Sept. 7 [2007] people are encouraged to wear teal for "Teal Time Day." Think of it as the ovarian cancer version of a pink ribbon. Advocates and researchers at the University of Michigan [U-M] Comprehensive Cancer Center hope efforts like this will get people talking about ovarian cancer. What's there to say? Start with these eight things you need to know:

Key Points About Ovarian Cancer

1. Symptoms do exist. Bloating, pelvic or abdominal pain, difficulty eating, feeling full quickly, and frequent or urgent urinating are shown to be more common in women with ovarian cancer. These are vague symptoms and often mistaken for gastrointestinal problems. But if they persist for several days, get checked out by your gynecologist. "You can explain away these symptoms to yourself. But the only way to be sure it's nothing is to go get a pelvic exam," says J. Rebecca Liu, M.D., assistant professor of obstetrics and gynecology at the U-M Medical School and a gynecologic oncologist at the U-M Comprehensive Cancer Center.

2. There is no screening test for ovarian cancer, like a Pap smear or mammogram. The CA125 blood test measures the amount of a certain protein that's often elevated with ovarian cancer. But the test is not foolproof. "There are a lot of benign conditions that can cause higher levels of CA125," Liu says. Early detection is a key area of research. U-M researchers

> **FAST FACT**
>
> According to an article in the June 2007 *Obstetrical and Gynecological Survey,* more than 70 percent of women diagnosed with ovarian cancer are in the latest stage of the disease.

Pitfalls When Screening for Ovarian Cancer

1. A preinvasive precursor lesion (detectable precancerous cells) may not exist.
2. Rapid growth rate limits chance for early detection.
3. Poor positive predictive value of any screening test due to low incidence (of ovarian cancer in the general population).
4. False-positive screening results have adverse psychological and financial consequences for patients.
5. Invasive surgery required to confirm diagnosis.

Taken from: Armenian Medical Network, "Ovarian Cancer: Recognizing Early Symptoms Can Make a Difference," April 25, 2008. www.health.am/cr/more/ovarian-cancer-recognizing-early-symptoms.

are looking for markers in the blood that indicate ovarian cancer, an approach that could in time lead to a blood test to screen for ovarian cancer.

3. All women need yearly pelvic exams. Maybe your doctor says you don't need a Pap smear every year, but Pap tests just check for cervical abnormalities. A pelvic exam is not the same thing. In particular, older women should not discontinue their yearly gynecology visit as ovarian cancer is more likely to occur in women older than 60. "A pelvic exam is key because it's the best screening we have right now," Liu says.

4. Survival rates are significantly better when ovarian cancer is diagnosed in an early stage. With stage I ovarian cancer, the earliest stage, 95 percent of women are alive five years after diagnosis. Only 30 percent of women with stage III or IV ovarian cancer survive five years. More than 22,000 women will be diagnosed with ovarian cancer this year and more than 15,000 will die from the disease. Some 70 percent of women have advanced disease when they are diagnosed.

5. Ovarian cancer is difficult to treat because it's often resistant to current treatments. It may respond to chemotherapy drugs initially, but when it recurs—which it usually does—the cells will no longer be killed by that drug. Researchers are focusing on new molecularly targeted therapies that hone in on and destroy the cancer cells, and they hope this will overcome the resistance. A new clinical trial recently opened to patient accrual at U-M looking at whether the drug Avastin, which has

Symptoms of bloating, pelvic or abdominal pain, eating difficulties, and frequent urination are more common in women with ovarian cancer. (© BSIP/Photo Researchers, Inc.)

been successful for colon cancer, can improve survival in ovarian cancer.

6. *It's most common in older white women.* Most patients are older than 60 and post-menopausal. Women who have not had children are at higher risk. Women who have taken birth control for a number of years lower their risk.

7. *A small number of ovarian cancers are hereditary.* It's linked to the same genes that are linked to breast cancer, BRCA1 and BRCA2. If ovarian cancer runs in your family, particularly on your mother's side, and if family members were diagnosed at a young age, you might consider genetic testing.

8. *The best person to treat ovarian cancer is a gynecologic oncologist.* These specialists are skilled in the comprehensive management of female reproductive cancers, including surgery and chemotherapy. Studies have shown gynecologic oncologists are two to three times more likely to provide surgical care consistent with national guidelines. Women with ovarian cancer treated by gynecologic oncologists have 10 percent to 25 percent better survival rates than women treated by general oncologists or gynecologists. While your regular gynecologist can perform diagnostic tests, if you are diagnosed with ovarian cancer, you should see a gynecologic oncologist.

Symptom Check-List:

- Bloating
- Pelvic or abdominal pain
- Difficulty eating or feeling full quickly
- Urinary symptoms (urgency or frequency)
- Symptoms are persistent and represent a change from the normal

Women who experience these symptoms almost daily for more than a few weeks should visit their regular gynecologist.

Symptoms of Ovarian Cancer May Not Help with Early Detection

Ilana Cass and Beth Y. Karlan

In the following viewpoint Ilana Cass and Beth Y. Karlan, research-ers at the Women's Cancer Research Institute at Cedars-Sinai Medical Center, argue that knowing some of the symptoms of ovar-ian cancer has limited use. In contrast, Mary Anne Rossing and her colleagues published a study in the *Journal of the American Cancer Institute* in 2010 reporting that knowing the symptoms of the dis-ease can save lives. When the disease is diagnosed early enough, women are more likely to be cured. Cass and Karlan assert that symptom recognition, while important, does not increase survival odds in the general population but might be used as a tool to help women with family histories of ovarian cancer. Cass and Karlan acknowledge that Rossing's study highlights the fact that the dis-ease does have symptoms, but they contend that better diagnostic tools, not symptom recognition, are needed to truly improve ovar-ian cancer cure rates.

SOURCE: Ilana Cass and Beth Y. Karlan, "Ovarian Cancer Symptoms Speak Out—but What Are They Really Saying?," *Journal of the American Cancer Institute,* vol. 102, no. 4. Copyright © 2010 by the Oxford University Press Journals. All rights reserved. Reproduced by permission.

It used to be accepted that ovarian cancer was a "silent killer." However, recent data have reproducibly demonstrated that the vast majority of patients with ovarian cancer have symptoms for at least several months before their diagnosis. A consensus statement encouraged recognition of a symptom complex including early satiety [feeling full quickly], bloating, abdominal and/or pelvic pain, and urinary changes as an aid in the diagnosis of ovarian cancer. The statement was endorsed by the American Cancer Society, the Society of Gynecologic Oncologists, and the Gynecologic Cancer Foundation in hopes that symptom recognition by patients and physicians would translate into earlier diagnosis and ultimately an improvement in overall survival. To date, there are limited data to suggest that symptom recognition can identify patients with early-stage ovarian cancer.

Identifying the Symptoms

The [2010] study by [Mary Anne] Rossing et al. in this issue of the *Journal [of the American Cancer Institute]* puts the symptom index to the test to see whether it can "down stage" ovarian cancer. The authors conducted in-person interviews with 812 case patients who had been diagnosed with ovarian cancer and 1,313 population-based control subjects from Western Washington state. Information was gathered retrospectively to reflect specific symptoms that these women might have experienced before the date of diagnosis (case patients) or before an assigned comparable reference date (control subjects). Categories of symptoms were drawn from the symptoms index described by [Barbara] Goff et al. and the ovarian cancer consensus criteria. The authors used an approximation of these guidelines to define a positive index if any symptom was present daily for at least 1 week with an onset of less than 12 months before diagnosis or the reference date. The authors further analyzed the types of symptoms by surgico-pathological features of the tumor including

Symptoms of Ovarian Cancer

Recent studies have shown that the following symptoms are much more likely to occur in women with ovarian cancer than in woman in the general population:

* Bloating
* Pelvic or abdominal pain
* Difficulty eating or feeling full quickly
* Urinary symptoms (urgency or frequency) . . .

Several other symptoms have also been commonly reported by women with ovarian cancer. They include:

* Fatigue
* Indigestion
* Back pain
* Pain with intercourse
* Constipation
* Menstrual irregularities

However, these other symptoms alone are not as useful in identifying ovarian cancer. That's because they are also found in equal frequency in women in the general population who do not have ovarian cancer.

Taken from: The Gynecologic Cancer Foundation and Project Hope for Ovarian Cancer Research and Education, *Understanding Your Risk of Ovarian Cancer: A Woman's Guide*, 2009.

invasive vs. borderline tumors, FIGO (i.e., International Federation of Gynecology and Obstetrics) stage, and histological subtypes as a proposed pathway of tumorigenesis. In this model, type I invasive tumors are characterized by slow progression and type II lesions are characterized by early metastasis.

The pattern of symptoms reported among case patients and control subjects was similar to that reported in the literature. The study clearly demonstrates that symptoms associated with ovarian cancer were 10 times more likely to occur in women who were ultimately diagnosed with the disease and were present whether they had early-

or late-stage ovarian cancer. Symptoms did not discriminate between invasive and borderline tumors or between type I and type II tumors. Symptoms were reported as being present for a relatively short period irrespective of the stage of disease. Among patients with early-stage disease, approximately 27% had symptoms present for at least 5 months before diagnosis. Addition of neither stage nor age statistically significantly improved the positive predictive values for the symptom index, and ultimately, the authors determined that 100 symptomatic women would need to be evaluated to detect one with early-stage ovarian cancer.

The strengths of the study include the in-person interviews and the large number of ovarian cancer case patients. Notably, 220 case patients with early-stage invasive ovarian cancer were included in the analysis, which allows a more valid test of the study hypothesis that ovarian cancer symptoms can signal earlier-stage disease. The study expands upon prior data by providing the positive predictive value of the symptoms index in the general population, which is a more meaningful criterion to compare its performance with other ovarian cancer screening tools.

Study Limitations

The study design by Rossing et al. suffers from the same limitations as many previous studies that have relied upon the retrospective reporting of symptoms. Although the investigators attempted to interview both case patients and control subjects in a timely fashion relative to the date of diagnosis or an appointed reference date (mean delay = 9 months among case patients and 10 months among control subjects), the retrospective nature of the design raises some doubts. The inherent recall bias among women with ovarian cancer may have inflated the frequency of positive symptom scores in case patients compared with control subjects. Among control

A computed tomography scan of a woman's pelvic region reveals a large ovarian tumor (in red). The blue area is a buildup of fluid in the abdominal cavity, indicating that the cancer has spread to the lining of the abdominal cavity (© Du Cane Medical Imaging/ Photo Researchers, Inc.)

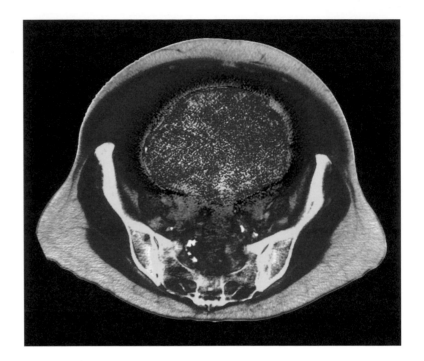

subjects, the ability of a woman to recall specific symptoms 10 months before the time of the interview is perhaps a bit optimistic. There is also the potential for survival bias in the cohort of case patients, given that most case patients were interviewed sometime after their diagnosis, which would have excluded women with more aggressive type II disease who succumbed to ovarian cancer before the interview.

The rationale for deviating from what has been defined as a positive symptom index in the literature is not clearly stated. The important difference in the definition of a "positive" index in the study by Rossing et al. is the frequency of the reported symptoms. Goff et al. defined a positive symptom index if a woman had symptoms that occurred more than 12 times per month. The symptom index criteria resulted from a logistic regression analysis of more than 20 symptoms that were validated by prospectively surveying case patients with ovarian cancer and control subjects before surgery or ultrasound or during surveillance in an early-detection program for ovarian cancer. The lower frequency of symptoms that was required by Rossing et al. may explain the higher sensitivity in that study than in other studies.

The exceedingly low estimated positive predictive values of a positive symptom index in the study by Rossing et al. is not surprising, given the high frequency of presentation with advanced-stage and the low prevalence of ovarian cancer in the general population. Even when the authors restricted their analysis to patients with early-stage disease, neither the type nor the duration that symptoms were present resulted in a predictive value of any real utility in the detection of ovarian cancer.

The study by Rossing et al. further debunks the falsehood that ovarian cancer is a "silent disease" and continues to raise awareness regarding the symptoms of ovarian cancer. Despite the discouraging conclusion that enhanced symptom recognition is unable to detect early-stage disease, the study provides further validation that ovarian cancer has specific symptoms in the vast majority of patients—whether they have early- or late-stage disease. How this knowledge should affect health-care decisions needs to be further evaluated in the context of a prospective clinical trial. Given the low prevalence of ovarian cancer, the positive symptom index had sensitivity and specificity rates that were similar to other screening tests that have been studied in the general population and judged to be inadequate. These symptoms may be more useful as a first step in a triage scheme for ovarian cancer detection in a high-risk hereditary cancer population that has a higher prevalence of disease. Even if the positive symptom index did not lead to "down staging" of the ovarian cancers in this study, it is plausible that earlier recognition and evaluation of these symptoms may affect disease outcome by decreasing the

FAST FACT

As reported by the Women's Cancer Network in 2010, the average woman has a one in seventy lifetime risk of developing ovarian cancer.

tumor burden at diagnosis, which has been shown to enhance patient survival.

Importantly, these findings remind us that wide recognition of symptoms alone will not incrementally improve the overall survival from ovarian cancer. Rather, they highlight the urgent need to develop better molecular markers and improved imaging modalities for ovarian cancer screening. The recognition of specific symptoms associated with ovarian cancer has value. However, to truly affect the cure of ovarian cancer, we need better diagnostic tools for asymptomatic women.

A previous American study that examined this issue, the Gynecologic Oncology Group's Protocol 80, closed after 2 years, having only enrolled 2 patients.

"Historically, primary surgery has a very important role in the treatment of ovarian cancer, and there are some biases on the part of physicians [in the United States]," said Dr. Bookman about the failure of the earlier study. "The new results are very compelling and could change clinical practice. The results should make doctors more comfortable with this approach," he added.

Diagnosing Ovarian Cancer

Ovarian cancer is difficult to diagnose until it has spread either via the lymph system or by direct extension to other organs or tissues.

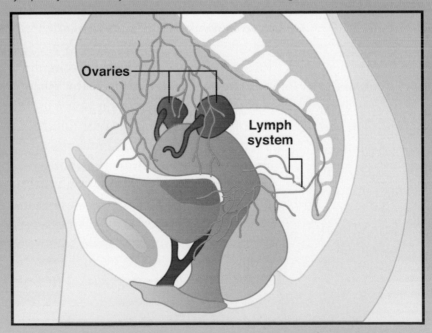

Taken from: *MedicineWorld* (blog), "Preferred Method of Treatment for Advanced Ovarian Cancer," 2011.
http://medicineworld.org/news/ovariannews.html.

In an interview with *Medscape Oncology*, Dr. Vergote agreed. "In Europe, about 25% of the patients [are] already treated with neoadjuvant chemotherapy. This study will and should change the standard globally for patients with very advanced stage IIIC and IV disease," he said.

The results were not surprising to Dr. Vergote but might be to others. "Many other experts, especially in the US, had their doubts about this," he said.

Dr. Vergote made the study presentation in Bangkok on behalf of his fellow investigators from the European Organization for Research and Treatment of Cancer–Gynaecological Cancer Group (EORTC–GCG) and the National Cancer Institute Canada–Clinical Trial Group (NCIC–CTG).

Reduction in Complications

Study participants with stage IIIC/IV ovarian, peritoneal, and fallopian tube carcinoma were randomized to receive either primary debulking surgery (followed by 6 cycles of platinum-based chemotherapy, which was mostly paclitaxel/carboplatin) or interval debulking surgery (which was preceded and followed by 3 cycles of the chemotherapy).

The median follow-up for all participants was 4.8 years. For the primary—and interval—debulking-surgery groups of the study, median overall survival (29 vs. 30 months) and progression-free survival (both 12 months) were similar in an intention-to-treat analysis.

However, reductions in complications were observed in the interval debulking-surgery group, including a statistically significant reduction in postoperative deaths (2.7% in the primary cohort vs 6% in the interval cohort). The other reductions included postoperative fever, grade 3/4 (8% vs 2%); hemorrhage, grade 3/4 (7% vs 1%); and blood clots (2.4% vs 0.3%).

FAST FACT

Elise Everett, of the University of Virginia Medical Center in Charlottesville, found that administering chemotherapy before surgery for ovarian cancer improved the success of optimal tumor removal by more than 30 percent.

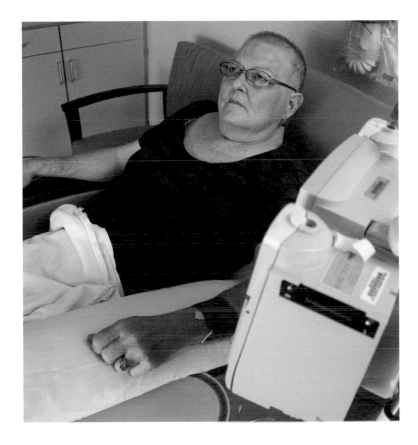

A woman undergoes chemotherapy prior to ovarian cancer surgery. Presurgical chemotherapy has improved the success of tumor removal by more than 30 percent. (© Norma Jean Gargasz/ Alamy)

"Interval cytoreductive surgery is at least as good as the old way and potentially safer with regard to risks of surgery," said Dr. Bookman.

However, there is one caveat to the study. "Chemotherapy before surgery should not be used in patients with less than FIGO [International Federation of Gynecology and Obstetrics] stage IIIC ovarian cancer or small IIIC ovarian cancers, as these patients were not well represented in the study," said Dr. Vergote.

Optimal Tumor Removal Still Matters More than Surgical Timing

In a multivariate analysis [involving more than one variable] by the investigators, optimal debulking surgery [surgically removing as much of the tumor as possible] was the strongest independent prognostic factor for overall survival among the study participants in both groups. Other significant prognostic factors included: histological [tissue] type, largest tumor size at randomization and disease stage.

Optimal debulking to no residual tumor should remain the goal of every surgical effort, noted Dr. Vergote. The timing of this procedure (primary or interval) "does not seem to play a role," he said.

With regard to surgical results, the patients who underwent interval debulking had better findings, with 53% having no residual tumors and 82% having tumors of less than 1 cm after surgery, compared with 21% and 46% of the primary debulking patients, respectively. "The masses were significantly smaller after chemotherapy. This makes the surgery easier," said Dr. Vergote.

Dr. Bookman also noted that this phase 3 study, which had more than 700 patients, was powered "to make sure that interval surgery was not worse than primary surgery," which is a "noninferiority" design. Only 400 patients were needed for a more traditional, "superiority" design, he said.

International Relevance

"This study is important for patients throughout the world, as it validates the safety and efficacy of a new approach that can be applied in many settings where scheduling, resources, and/or clinical feasibility could limit availability of immediate front-line surgery," said Dr. Bookman in a statement.

Interval cytoreductive surgery is also currently the subject of the Chemotherapy or Upfront Surgery in Ovarian Cancer Patients (CHORUS) study in Canada and the United Kingdom, which are both countries with national health systems that can have scheduling backlogs for major surgeries such as cytoreduction, Dr. Bookman told *Medscape Oncology*.

Hormone Therapy Increases the Risk of Developing Ovarian Cancer

Kathleen Doheny

In the following viewpoint Kathleen Doheny, a regular contributor to the *Los Angeles Times*, *Shape*, and WebMD, reports on a study that confirms the link between hormone therapy and ovarian cancer. The results of the study, conducted by Lina Morch and colleagues at Rigshospitalet at Copenhagen University in Denmark, were published in a 2008 issue of the *Journal of the American Medical Association*. According to their findings, women who take hormone therapy to ease the symptoms of menopause are at an increased risk of developing ovarian cancer. Although the risk declines over time following stoppage of the treatment, the immediate risk can be up to 38 percent higher for women who use hormones than for women who do not. Doheny concludes that, as with most studies, Morch's findings are limited, but her study sheds new light on this potentially deadly connection.

SOURCE: Kathleen Doheny, "Hormone Therapy Raises Ovarian Cancer Risk," WebMD.com, July 14, 2009. Copyright © 2009 by WebMD.com. All rights reserved. Reproduced by permission.

Women who are on hormone therapy or who have used it in the recent past are at higher risk of ovarian cancer than women who have never been on hormone therapy, a new [2009] study shows.

The increase in risk was found regardless of the hormone dose or formulation, whether hormones were taken by mouth, transdermal patch, or vaginally, or whether the treatment included just estrogen or estrogen and progestin, the researchers say.

The study confirms earlier research linking hormone therapy and ovarian cancer, but the new study is believed to be the largest and most detailed study to date on the topic, says the study's lead author Lina Morch, a researcher at Rigshospitalet, Copenhagen University in Denmark.

"Our study underlines that postmenopausal hormones increase the risk for ovarian cancer," she tells WebMD in an email interview. "Furthermore, this study suggests that no type of hormone seems safe regarding the risk of ovarian cancer—even at use below four years the risk is increased." Some previous research had not found an increased cancer risk with hormone use of less than five years.

Both estrogen alone and combination therapy that adds progestin boosted risk, Morch says. Her study is published in the *Journal of the American Medical Association.*

Ovarian Cancer and Hormones

In the study, Morch and her team evaluated more than 909,000 Danish women, ages 50 to 79, who were on national Danish registers. After an average of eight years of follow-up, 3,068 cases of ovarian cancer were found. At the end of the study, 63% of the women were never-users of hormone therapy and 9% [were] current users.

Compared to never-users, current hormone therapy users had an overall 38% increased risk of ovarian cancer.

Put another way: for every 8,300 women on hormone therapy per year, one extra case of ovarian cancer could be attributed to hormone therapy.

Risk did decline in past users as the years of being hormone-free increased. By the time past users had been off hormone therapy for two years, their risk of ovarian cancer was about the same as for non-users, Morch found. By the time women had been off the hormone therapy for more than six years, the risk of ovarian cancer was nearly 40% less in these past users than the never-users. Morch

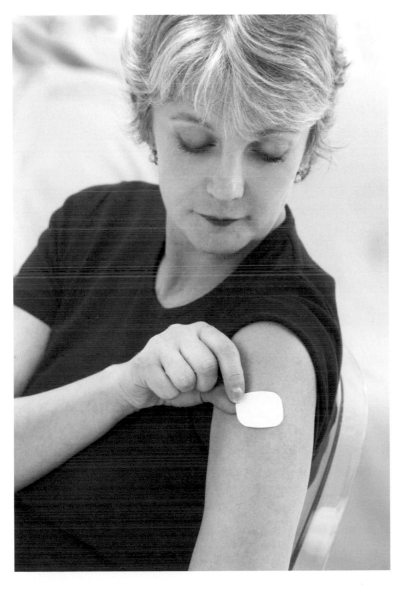

A 2009 study in Denmark has found that women who use or who have recently used hormone therapy are at a higher risk of ovarian cancer. (© Lea Paterson/Photo Researchers, Inc.)

says that finding is based on a low number of women who had quit hormone therapy for more than six years. "What is important is the risk declines in former users with increasing time since last use," she says.

For those currently on hormone therapy, the risk of getting ovarian cancer didn't differ much among the various therapies, doses, or administration, Morch found.

"Ovarian cancer is among the most lethal of gynecologic cancers," Morch says. "The five-year survival rates are 40%." To complicate the issue, ovarian cancer is difficult to detect, and thus often not found until it is in advanced stages.

Previous research has found that current use of hormones raises ovarian cancer risk by 30% compared with no hormone use, with the risk of estrogen-only therapy sometimes found to be higher than combined therapy.

"This study supports an approximately similar increased risk for ovarian cancer disregarding the hormone type," she says.

This year, 21,550 new cases of ovarian cancer are expected in the U.S., with an estimated 14,600 deaths from the disease, according to American Cancer Society estimates.

Second Opinion

"It's a well done study," says Andrew Li, MD, a gynecologic oncologist at Cedars-Sinai Medical Center, Los Angeles, who reviewed the study for WebMD. "Their findings are in line with what other people report," says Li, who is also an assistant clinical professor of obstetrics and gynecology at the University of California Los Angeles' David Geffen School of Medicine.

Like most research, the study has limitations that may have affected the results, Li says, and the authors also acknowledge this. Among the limitations are that the researchers didn't adjust for age at menopause or use of birth control pills; birth control pill use and early natural menopause both reduce ovarian cancer risk.

Prescriptions for Hormone Therapy, 2006–2010

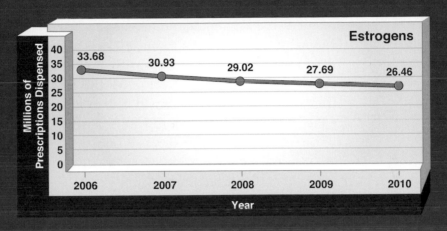

Estrogens

33.68 30.93 29.02 27.69 26.46

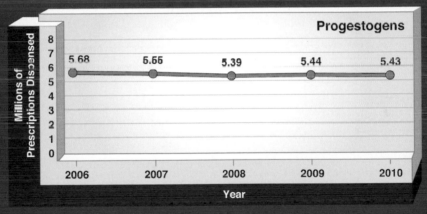

Progestogens

5.68 5.55 5.39 5.44 5.43

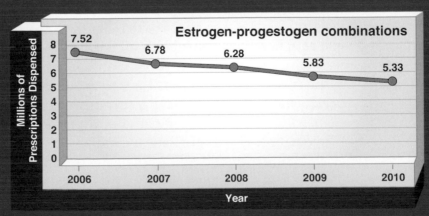

Estrogen-progestogen combinations

7.52 6.78 6.28 5.83 5.33

The main contribution of the new study is to look at large numbers of women who took different types of hormone therapy and determine which type or types carry risk, says Shelley Tworoger, PhD, an assistant professor of medicine and epidemiology at the Harvard School of Medicine and School of Public Health, who has also published her research on hormone therapy and ovarian cancer risk. "The real contribution [of the new study] is that the combined regimen also increases the risk of ovarian cancer," she says. In her research, Tworoger found that estrogen-only therapy boosted risk and a suggestion of an increased risk with estrogen and progestin therapy.

The new research basically confirms what has been shown in previous studies, says Corrado Altomare, MD, senior director of global-medical affairs for Wyeth Pharmaceuticals in Collegeville, Pa. "This finding doesn't really change what we know," he tells WebMD. "We actually have a warning in our label about ovarian cancer."

Wyeth's label summarizes the risks found for ovarian cancer with hormone use, using information from various studies.

The best advice for women? "If a woman has a special predisposition for ovarian cancer, she should consider not taking hormones," Morch says. Past users, she says, can be reassured that their risk declines to that of never users after being off the therapy for two years.

Even with the link to ovarian cancer, Morch says, she is not saying hormone therapy should never be used. "Hormones may still have a therapeutic place in women with severe perimenopausal symptoms, and among women going into premature menopause," she says.

Women should talk to their doctor about hormone use, Li says, so the decision can be based on individual risk factors and medical history.

FAST FACT

A 2010 report by European Prospective Investigation into Cancer and Nutrition found that women who use hormone therapy are at greater risk for developing ovarian cancer, regardless of other characteristics.

Oral Contraceptives Reduce the Long-Term Risk of Developing Ovarian Cancer

Addison Greenwood

Addison Greenwood is a science writer at the National Cancer Institute. In the following viewpoint he explains the findings of a study conducted by the Collaborative Group on Epidemiological Studies of Ovarian Cancer. The study, published in the *Lancet*, revealed that the use of oral contraceptives lowers the risk of ovarian cancer. In fact, oral contraceptives offer protection against the disease for years after discontinued use; in addition, the longer oral contraceptives are used, the greater the ovarian cancer risk reduction. Greenwood concludes by noting that the risk factors for long-term use of oral contraceptives were not taken into consideration in the study; therefore, it is not recommended that oral contraceptives be prescribed to all women as a means of preventing ovarian cancer.

Since they were first licensed nearly 50 years ago, birth control pills containing estrogen have prevented some 200,000 cases of ovarian cancer worldwide, estimate the authors of a study published January

SOURCE: Addison Greenwood, "Oral Contraceptives Reduce Long-Term Risk of Ovarian Cancer," *NCI Cancer Bulletin*, vol. 5, no. 3, February 5, 2008.

26 [2008] in *The Lancet*. Further, in the absence of having taken oral contraceptives, half of these women would have died of the disease.

The researchers showed that oral contraceptives (OCs) continue to confer protection for years—even decades—after women stop using them. Thus, they surmise, "the number of ovarian cancers prevented [will] rise over the next few decades" to at least 30,000 each year.

> **FAST FACT**
>
> The Yale Cancer Center reports that the decrease in risk of developing ovarian cancer may last up to twenty-five years after the use of oral contraceptives has ended.

These figures emerge from a comprehensive meta-analysis based on prospective and case-control data from 45 epidemiological studies in 21 countries, mostly in Europe and the United States. "These findings set a new standard in prevention for a deadly cancer," wrote the editors of *The Lancet*, "and have important public health implications."

The results showed that women who had ever taken OCs were 27 percent less likely to develop ovarian cancer. The studies included 23,257 women with ovarian cancer, 31 percent of whom had taken OCs; of the 87,303 controls, 37 percent took OCs.

Surprising Findings

Two trends emerged that were really striking, according to Dr. Beth Karlan, editor-in-chief of *Gynecologic Oncology* and director of the Gilda Radner Cancer Detection Program at Cedars-Sinai Outpatient Cancer Center in Los Angeles. First, the longer OCs were used, the greater the ovarian cancer risk reduction, decreasing about 20 percent for each 5 years of use.

The second clear trend was the duration of the protective effects, which lasted long after women had stopped using OCs. For each 5 years of use, risk of developing ovarian cancer was reduced 29 percent in the first 10 years after stopping. The risk reduction was still significant though smaller (19 percent) for years 10–20, and smaller still (15 percent) 20–29 years after discontinuation.

Another feature of these results is their uniformity. OCs seem to protect against nearly all types of epithelial and nonepithelial tumors, with the possible exception of mucinous ovarian cancer (which accounted for only 12 percent of cases studied in the meta-analysis). *The Lancet* editorial points out that the results show "the benefits of oral contraceptives are independent of the preparation [estrogen dose], and vary little by ethnic origin, parity, family history of breast cancer, body-mass index, and use of hormone replacement therapy."

Representatives from nearly all of these studies—including Drs. Patricia Hartge, James Lacey, Louise Brinton, and Robert Hoover from the Epidemiology and Biostatistics Program in NCI's Division of Cancer Epidemiology and Genetics (DCEG)—worked together to ensure the integrity of the analysis, forming the Collaborative

A 2008 study indicated that the use of oral contraceptives has been found to reduce the long-term risk of ovarian cancer. (© David L. Moore/Alamy)

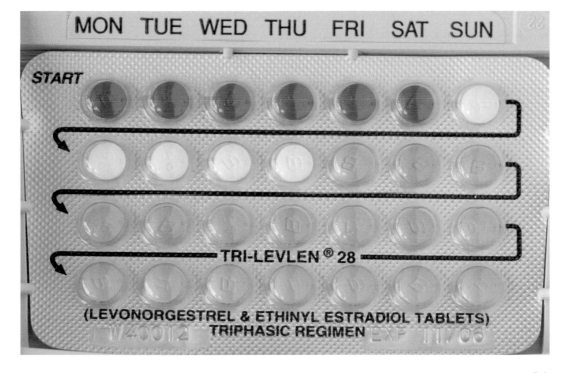

Birth Control Pill Use and Risk of Ovarian Cancer

Relative Risk of Ovarian Cancer

Years Using Birth Control Pills	Value
Never taken	1
Less than 1 year	1
1–4 years	0.78
5–9 years	0.64
10–14 years	0.56
15 years or more	0.42

Taken from: *Cancer News in Context* (blog), "Oral Contraceptives Reduce Cancer Deaths," March 30, 2010. www.cancernewsincontext.org/2010/03/oral-contraceptives-reduce-cancer.html.

Group on Epidemiological Studies of Ovarian Cancer, under the leadership of Dr. Valerie Beral and colleagues at Oxford University's Cancer Research UK Epidemiology Unit.

Possible Limitations

The absence of proven screening methods for ovarian cancer make these findings all the more welcome. But the issue is not straightforward, because calculating "the net effect on women's health is fraught with uncertainties," wrote Drs. Eduardo L. Franco and Eliane Duarte-Franco of McGill University in Montreal in a comment accompanying the article. They went on to list possible side effects of OCs as increased risk of thromboembolism, heart disease, migraine, liver disease, and several other relatively uncommon conditions.

The analyses were not focused on comparing the benefits and risks of OCs, explains DCEG's Dr. Brinton, but only examined their effect on ovarian cancer risk. In the absence of detailed risk-benefit data, including currently unknown risks, such as cancers in women who have taken OCs and later take long-term hormone replacement therapy, she says, "This meta-analysis does not recommend widespread prescription of OCs as a preventative measure against ovarian cancer."

Dr. Beral commented that while OCs may pose a slight increased risk of breast and cervical cancer, the effect is small and disappears once the drugs are no longer being used, as contrasted with the ongoing protective effect against ovarian cancer.

Dr. Karlan added, "Ovarian cancer remains a disease with a high mortality due [mainly] to our inability to reliably diagnose it at an early stage. Women are concerned about this risk." She noted that it is important for women to be aware that OCs reduce that risk when discussing their contraceptive choices with their health care providers.

CHAPTER 3

Personal Experiences with Ovarian Cancer

Life After Ovarian Cancer Can Be Frightening

Jane Kelly

In the following viewpoint Jane Kelly, the author of two books and many articles, reveals her struggle with ovarian cancer. Although she is considered cured of the disease, she lives in fear that it will return. She was diagnosed after the cancer had spread to her lymph nodes, which means she was in stage IV. The long-term survival rate of patients with stage IV ovarian cancer is poor. According to Kelly, her doctors agree that her chances of survival beyond a few years are low. Meanwhile, though she fears its recurrence, her experience with cancer has made her appreciate life more. Kelly lives in London and blogs about life with ovarian cancer.

While the nation slumped in front of the TV over Christmas I was tentatively feeling my groin for lumps. As my mother hunted through the TV schedules to find the news, surprised to be seeing again everything she'd enjoyed in the Seventies, I was

Photo on facing page. For many patients, including this teen, life after contracting any type of cancer is pervaded with the fear that the cancer will recur. (© National Geographic Image Collection/Alamy)

panicking quietly about a slight ache in my diaphragm. If my cancer had returned, where was it? With not one medical book in the house, I sat unseeing in front of the telly, my mind teeming with dire fantasies.

In the daytime, out walking, I wondered if I could estimate how near or far I was from death by looking at how near or far were other people on the pavement. Quite a distance behind, I saw a figure slowly pushing a bike. A young man with a fretful child in a pushchair got between us. When I looked back, the figure with the bike had gone. I took that as a good omen.

Life After Cancer

This is my life now after cancer: superstitious, nonsensical bargaining games and constant, obsessive checking. When I feel tired I'm sure I can feel lumps everywhere; they've gone the next morning. I eat so much broccoli and curly kale, with their allegedly cancer-fighting properties, that I feel bloated, but then wonder—is the bloating caused by the greens, or is it cancer? I won't know until my next test in two weeks, an agonisingly long time away.

I was diagnosed with stage four ovarian cancer in April last year [2010] after a swollen lymph node appeared in my groin. I was 53. They operated in early May. The disease had spread to three lymph nodes. "This is a Rottweiler not a poodle," my consultant boomed bombastically.

I expected the doctors to scrape out, blitz and destroy the cancer, which they did. Chemotherapy followed and I had no serious problems with it. Coming to the end of chemo felt like a victory and all my relations and friends shared in the relief.

My last scan, at the end of September, was all clear. I had a letter saying there was "no residual disease." So I should be happy. By their skill the doctors saved me, but by their manner they have crippled me with fear. At my last consultation the medic warned me that as my cancer had been aggressive it might come back within two years, but admitted that no one knew what would happen. "Too early in your treatment to tell," she said.

That was the moment I realised everything was beginning, not ending. "I know that's tough psychologically," she said. "Check your body regularly and hope for the best."

Seeking Reassurance

Needing more reassurance I went back to the clinic the next day, and saw a different doctor. "It will be back between two months to a year," he told me jovially as if it was a good joke. "Only between two to four percent of patients don't see their cancer return. It's very unlikely that the chemo will work. Fingers crossed," he said with a bumptious grin.

I went home that day robbed of all hope; life had changed completely.

On the bus I felt I was about to burst with tears. That doctor had about as much empathy as Simon Cowell: seeing him was like having a bad accident. I had the operation on the day of the general election; now it seemed I might not outlive the Coalition.

From then on I felt fragile with fear, as though waiting for the cancer tsunami to roar back and engulf me. My kindly GP was so concerned about the state I was in that he rang the hospital. He spoke to a doctor who supported the grim prognosis, based on statistics, the science of probability.

According to them, chemo for ovarian cancer stage 4 has a 98 per cent failure rate. A friend from the clinic said her doctor had said it was 50/50. We both still cling to that.

Percentages rattle round in my head. How do you live with this uncertainty? Medics don't give any advice about that.

> **FAST FACT**
>
> According to a study published in a 2007 issue of the *Annals of Internal Medicine,* the median life expectancy for patients with stage IV ovarian cancer is 2.95 years.

A Glimmer of Hope

A hundred years ago, kindly patrician doctors kept information back; now they give you the full works, hitting patients over the head with worst-case-scenarios, with apparently no scope for anything in-between. Perhaps they are afraid of giving false hopes, being "blamed" if you don't get well; or perhaps it's down to some politically correct idea of patients "owning" their own illness.

David Servan-Schreiber's book, *Anticancer*, describes his fight with an aggressive brain tumour, diagnosed when he was 31; he is now 49 and in good health. He writes about the dreaded survival statistics—and how they're just that: averages, means, numbers. He believes we can

The author, paralyzed by fear that her cancer would return, took heart from the controversial book *Anticancer* by David Servan-Schreiber (pictured), which describes Servan-Schreiber's recovery from an aggressive brain tumor through a healthy diet, exercise, and stress reduction. (© AP Images/John Heller)

transcend the numbers by following an "anti-cancer life-style," through diet, exercise, and stress reduction. Critics say he is giving cancer patients false hopes, but he accuses oncologists of giving people "false hopelessness," sapping them of the energy needed for recovery.

My energy was certainly sapped by the news that the chemo probably won't work, and that in all likelihood I face a chronic illness, which means a life where chunks of the year are taken up by intravenous drips and nauseating drugs. This news was delivered, by the male doctors particularly, with a kind of glib nonchalance.

I might be lily-livered, but the lack of what used to be called "the bedside manner," has left me crushed. People say, don't worry, anyone could be hit by a bus tomorrow; but cancer statistics are about calculating the odds, which the doctors insist are very poor.

This sense of fighting an implacable enemy is part of being in the modern "cancer community," where we are termed, "survivors." When we meet, this cancer community, our first talk is about the possible (and so far unproven) value of Omega 3, goji berries, Montmorency cherries, nut milk and Manuka honey. We believe (rightly or wrongly) that processed sugar will feed our cancers. We envy those who have made it to old age.

Reaching Out to Others

Of course, bad luck strikes almost everyone at some time and struggling against the odds does have its rewards. I have changed since I realised that time may be short. Changed, not just in my hair coming more wiry than before, and in my eating allegedly cancer-fighting different foods, but in my attitude.

I have more interest in people of all kinds, more desire to get involved. I am grateful old friends have reappeared and delightful new people have come into my life. Everything and everyone has more value. Ordinary, everyday things like going on the coffee morning rota at my church have become a special pleasure.

My faith in a higher spiritual power flickers; when it goes out I realise how scared I am, when it returns I have something beautiful to hold on to.

At present there seems to be no end to this anxiety but I know that things might get better with time. If I survive for five years and look towards ten, when the check-ups will have stopped, I can regard the whole thing as a tiresome job, from which I will one day retire. Who knows, in that time, the doctors, brilliant and driven as they are, might have found a cure.

No one knows what will happen—the only certain thing said to me so far.

Paying Attention to Your Body Is the Best Defense Against Ovarian Cancer

Holly Miller

Holly Miller was diagnosed with ovarian cancer in 2009. In the following viewpoint she describes the fortunate circumstances of her diagnosis, her journey to being cancer free, and her life afterward. She saw her doctor for a routine yearly exam and complained of chronic fatigue and irregular periods. Her doctor sent her for an ultrasound, which revealed a tumor on her ovary. After surgery and chemotherapy, she was told that she was cancer free. Since that time she has become an ovarian cancer activist. She concludes her story with a list of ways readers can help friends battling cancer.

O ctober 2009: Two days before leaving for a trip to Alaska with my husband, I found out that I had a cyst on my right ovary. Shortly after returning home and having surgery, the date of October 27 will forever stick out in my mind. That was the day my doctor said, "You have ovarian cancer."

My cancer journey began with a routine yearly exam. What began with, "is there anything going on that I need to be aware of" question from my doctor turned into "it's probably nothing but let me schedule an ultrasound just to be sure." My complaint to her was that I had been experiencing what I thought was severe fatigue over the past few months. I would be ready to take a nap at 2 P.M. and not get up until the next morning, that's how tired I was. I thought this to be strange because I exercised regularly and ate healthy. I also told her my menstrual cycle was out of whack. Dr. Rebecca Walker was just the beginning of many doctors that would, in a sense, save my life. The ultrasound revealed a tumor on my right ovary.

Surgery was scheduled to remove it. I awoke to the news that she not only had to remove my right ovary, but right fallopian tube as well. She informed me that she, along with Dr. David Martin, took eight samples throughout my abdomen because they had found some suspicious spots. One thing led to another and a complete hysterectomy was done on November 12, 2009. On Thanksgiving that same year I collapsed in my garage because of a massive infection from my surgery, something that can happen after what my body had been through. I landed in the Critical Care Unit and spent a week in the hospital recovering.

The circumstances of my diagnosis were a complete fluke. Had I not been proactive in telling my doctor what was going on with my body she may not have ever suggested the ultrasound. In hindsight I had been having symptoms for quite some time; I just didn't know they were symptoms. I had been experiencing fatigue and abnormal monthly cycles but I also experienced bloating and feeling full quickly after eating. Many of the symptoms for ovarian cancer are things we as women feel all of the time and attribute to

FAST FACT

Researchers at the University of Pennsylvania report that in 2010 there was one death from ovarian cancer every forty-five minutes in the United States.

simply being a woman. Paying attention to your body is the best defense against ovarian cancer. Unlike breast cancer, with ovarian cancer there is no lump you can feel.

Facing Reality

My husband, Bradly, and I have been married since 2001 and have known each other since we were 15 years old. Before cancer crept its way into our lives, we had always hoped of having children. My diagnosis of Stage III ovarian cancer at the age of 33 completely closed that door. I never thought I would have to deal with a complete hysterectomy, much less cancer at my age.

I could not put what had happened to us into words. I totally avoided the ringing phone, not quite ready to face my new reality. I did have to watch Bradly fight for words as he tearfully explained what was going on. I remember watching him search for the right words to say and having tears in his eyes when he told my friends and loved ones the news.

January 2010: After severe weight loss due to my surgeries and post-surgery infection, a port was placed in my chest and I began 28 weeks of chemotherapy. I've always heard that a support system is essential when battling something so huge—and boy is it ever. During my battle I was comforted by support ranging from numerous cards, letters and e-mails to delicious meals provided by my girlfriends and neighbors. I had planned on writing thank you cards to everyone who has touched my life this past year, but I have realized what a gargantuan un dertaking that would be not just on my part, but also for that of the U.S. Postal Service! . . .

I would also love to see everyone who took such great care of us so I could thank them. The oncology nurses at Parkwest Medical Center especially rock! Dr. David Martin and Dr. Brooke Saunders along with their staff and nurses were terrific and very compassionate to me. Although I have come so far this past year, anniversaries are every day for me. Little things trigger memories and the list is too long to share. I believe it has to get better with time. On my "cancerversary" this past October, my Facebook status read, "A year ago today I was diagnosed with ovarian cancer. If I've learned nothing over the past year, I've learned that I'm a SURVIVOR."

Fighting a Long Battle

Looking back on my experience with the big "C", many advertising slogans have hit home. Nike's "Just Do It" for obvious reasons. It comes down to fight or flight when you're hit with a life-changing diagnosis and "Just Do It" applied to me in so many ways. Surgery: done. More IV's: done. More drugs: done. More chemo: done. L'Oreal's slogan of "Because I'm Worth It" is a good one in a hilarious kind of way. The whole "sass your way through chemo" is a mind game that if played well is more of a survival technique than anything. You better believe I'm worth it! The best one yet that hits home for all of us who have had cancer, is the American Cancer Society's "The Official Sponsor of Birthdays." There were so many times during the year after I was diagnosed that I wondered if I would be able to see another one.

If anything, I think having cancer taught me to cherish every moment. I have such a desire to "live" that I haven't really given my body time to rest. I guess I'm addicted to feeling alive again. I love the sense of accomplishment that overwhelms me when I do something that seemed totally out of my reach last year.

That being said, I've tackled a lot this year that I'm very proud of—including rock climbing in Colorado in September 2010 with others who had cancer. For those of you who may know me, I hate asking for help. The climb forced me to kick that to the curb. Who would have thought that I would actually enjoy not only the climb, but also the soreness it brought on the next day!

Following her cancer surgery, the author participated in rock-climbing activities with other cancer survivors. (© Stock Connection Blue/Alamy)

Someone asked me to be "real" about what was going on with me. "Real" is avoiding the ringing phone because you just can't bear to answer the question "how are you feeling" one more time. "Real" is knowing how bad your weekend is going to be after having chemotherapy on Thursday, and "real" is me apologizing repeatedly to my husband because I can't have children. Fighting cancer is a battle. Not just physically, but also emotionally.

A co-worker of mine came up with the "Gone Teal" idea. After being diagnosed with a cancer that "no one my age gets diagnosed with" everyone began looking around and seeing pink. T-shirts were designed with the "Gone Teal—to support Holly Miller" slogan on the back and "peace, love, cure ovarian cancer" on the front. I've spotted the t-shirts out and about in Knoxville [Tennessee] and we have sent them as far away as Seattle and they've been worn as far away as Australia! It's amazing what can come from one diagnosis.

Now that I am a cancer survivor, I want to make an impact so that women everywhere will be proactive in their routine screenings so we can combat cancer. While fighting this battle, I have learned 21,880 women were expected to be diagnosed with ovarian cancer this year [2011] and 13,850 will die from it. A women's lifetime risk of having it is one in 67 which is pretty significant when you think of how many people we all know. Support ovarian cancer awareness and wear teal the first Friday of each month.

A Top 10 List for Friends Battling Cancer
1. Call them—Hearing a friend's voice is priceless.
2. Send a card—I still have every card that was sent to me.
3. Write a letter (or an e-mail)—I know it's time consuming, but time is all a chemo patient has when they're stuck on the couch or in the bed.
4. Stop by for a visit—Although I didn't always have much to say, having someone in the house was comforting.
5. Send food—Food is a MUST because cooking was the last thing on my mind when I was so very sick.
6. Send a Facebook message—I looked forward to this every day!
7. Give them a hug (cancer's not contagious)—Hugs almost always made me cry, but I needed them.
8. Offer to clean their house—I was too exhausted and wiped out to simply dust the table in front of me, much less vacuum the house.

9. Do something drastic—While I was in the hospital, my co-workers decorated my house for Christmas. It wouldn't have gotten done otherwise, and when I saw it I cried like a baby. It was the best present ever!

10. Be their friend—Having a good support system is vital. Be there for your friend who was diagnosed in any way you can. They will need you to lean on and most of all—they will need you to make them laugh when times get tough

Ovarian Cancer Does Not Have to Mean Infertility

Missy Light Dougherty

Missy Light Dougherty is an ovarian cancer survivor. Her road to recovery was a delicate one because she longed to preserve her fertility so that she and her husband could have more children. After her diagnosis, she sought a second opinion about the kind of surgery she needed. In the end her doctor had to remove only one of her ovaries. She eventually gave birth to a little girl, and at the time of her daughter's arrival, Dougherty was cancer free. Since then she has joined the fight against ovarian cancer and offers other women hope.

The summer of 2007 was supposed to be like any other summer. My husband, son and I would be spending most of the summer in Sea Isle, but I started to not feel like myself. I was more tired than usual and began having symptoms consistent with irritable bowel syndrome and a urinary tract infection.

I began seeing different doctors and tried various medications. I even cut back work, but nothing seemed to help. I knew something was wrong, but no one had the answers. Finally a CT scan of my abdomen and pelvic region detected an ovarian cyst and two small stones. This marked the beginning of a long journey.

The Diagnosis and Surgery

My doctor was reluctant to operate and suggested that we monitor the situation instead. I really wanted the surgery and in October, I had successful surgery to remove the cyst. Two days later, my doctor called with the pathology report and told me that it wasn't just a cyst.

It turned out that I had cancer in my left ovary, which is typically treated with a total hysterectomy. My doctor told me that ovarian cancer is often hard to detect because the symptoms match those of other ailments, just like what I had been experiencing. This news was very upsetting since my husband and I had hoped to have more children.

We decided to get a second opinion. We met with a surgeon who offered to remove the left ovary, leaving my other ovary intact, as long as the disease had not spread. However, he informed us that he had never performed this procedure before and our confidence in a successful outcome quickly diminished.

> **FAST FACT**
>
> In 2006 the American Cancer Society stated that having a child does not increase a woman's risk of cancer recurring.

Finally, a friend in the medical field suggested I go to Fox Chase [Cancer Center in Pennsylvania]. She thought I would be in good hands given my unique situation. There we met Dr. Mark Morgan, a surgeon at Fox Chase who had successfully operated on younger women and was able to preserve their fertility. We quickly put our faith in his hands.

Dr. Morgan was able to remove the left ovary, keeping the right one intact. We knew going into surgery that there was no guarantee that this would preserve our

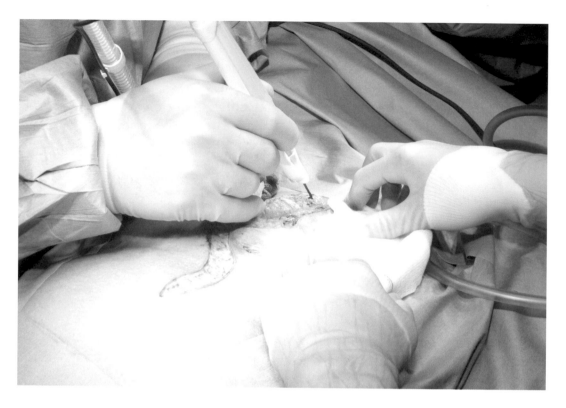

A surgeon makes an incision in the abdomen of a woman being operated on for ovarian cancer. (© Dr. P. Marazzi/Photo Researchers, Inc.)

ability to have more children. However, when I woke up from surgery, I saw my husband in tears and he told me that my cancer was caught early and we might be able to conceive another child.

I stayed at Fox Chase for a week and Dr. Morgan popped in frequently to check on me. I was so impressed with the nursing staff and how attentive they were to my needs. Then I received a call from my doctor who explained that I was at risk of the cancer spreading to my abdomen due to the fact that it had burst during the original surgery at my local hospital. So, I began chemotherapy at Fox Chase just before Christmas.

Trying Again

By March, my menstrual cycle had returned and by August, I was given a clean bill of health. My husband and I were given the "green-light" to try and have another baby.

Just before a follow-up appointment scheduled in October, I began feeling nauseated and tired again. My first thought was that the cancer had returned. It was at Fox Chase that I learned I was not sick, but pregnant! The first time I heard the baby's heartbeat, I cried like crazy. It was exactly one year after I had received my first dose of chemotherapy. On July 10, 2009, I gave birth to our beautiful daughter. We named her Molly, which means, gift of the sea. At Molly's birth I had no signs of cancer.

When I was initially diagnosed, I was introduced to the Sandy Rollman Foundation, which was my "lifeline" of support. The foundation is committed to educating women and doctors, advocating for early diagnostic testing, and raising funds to help advance research towards a cure. The people at the Foundation, especially co-founder Robin Cohen, made me believe I could win the battle and offered me so much hope for future days.

I've met so many women who have similar stories to mine. When I talked about how frustrating it was for me not to know what was wrong, they said, "Join the club." It showed me how important it is to raise awareness of the signs of ovarian cancer. My life has been touched by such amazing, strong people, and that has been a gift despite all that I went through. When our Rollman Foundation committee gets together for meetings, the room is hope-filled. There's a sense that we're going to fight this, and we're moving forward.

Surviving Aggressive Stage I Ovarian Cancer Can Be Done

Mia Aimaro Ogden

In the following viewpoint Mia Aimaro Ogden discusses her battle with an aggressive form of stage I ovarian cancer. She was on vacation with her husband when her stomach began to swell. Overnight it had become uncomfortably swollen, despite her efforts to exercise and eat well. Tests revealed a mass on her ovary, and after surgery to remove her ovaries and uterus, the diagnosis of cancer was confirmed. Ogden then had to undergo chemotherapy as an extra measure against the disease. The side effects of the treatment left her with hot flashes and no hair, but surviving a cancer diagnosis also gave her a new appreciation for life's small pleasures.

I was just 40 when I was diagnosed with ovarian cancer. That's pretty unusual—only 15% of cases occur in women below the age of 50. It's one of those diseases that's completely unsexy. It lacks the trendy factor: we don't have a poster girl like Kylie Minogue. Ask a

SOURCE: Mia Aimaro Ogden, "What It Feels Like to Survive Ovarian Cancer," *Sunday Times* (London), November 29, 2009. Copyright © 2009 by News International Syndication. All rights reserved. Reproduced by permission.

bunch of women what to look for with breast cancer and most will know at least a little. Ask them about ovarian cancer and the majority won't even have heard of it, let alone know what the symptoms are. I was one of those.

Sudden Symptoms

It happened really suddenly, and that's unusual, too: most women have a gradual build-up of symptoms over a long period. My husband, Jonathan, and I had been staying in London: we'd been out to lots of great restaurants, eaten heaps of good food, and the day we were coming home, I found I couldn't do up my trousers. But we were laughing: here was I, in first class, on the train back to Glasgow, with my gappy trousers, and, gosh, how much have we eaten?

When I woke up the following morning, my belly looked as if I was seven or eight months pregnant: it was huge. It happened just like that, in the space of 24 hours. I was a size 8, and I loved the body-con [body-conscious] look, so I would have noticed any swelling before. There was no pain, and I honestly thought I'd eaten too much. I had only one dress I could wear, an A-line that skimmed my enormous stomach. I persevered with this great belly for several days, but it was deeply uncomfortable. At night, I couldn't sleep, and my lower back became sore. I suppose it was what you feel like when you're pregnant. I walked to work every day—I'm an academic in linguistics at Glasgow University—which was about three miles. I even tried to run it off. But none of it made any difference.

I finally went to see my doctor, but I thought I was wasting his time: I didn't feel sick, no problems with my bowels. GPs have been criticised in the *British Medical Journal* recently for confusing the signs of ovarian cancer with irritable bowel syndrome, which may be why only 40% of women diagnosed survive beyond five years in Britain. Doctors don't know what they're looking for, so we aren't treated quickly enough. This country has one of the lowest survival rates in Europe. Thankfully, my GP knew better. He took one look at me and sent me to Glasgow Royal Infirmary A&E [Accident & Emergency Department] with a referral letter. There, they took an x-ray of my abdomen and admitted me.

Even then, I was still thinking: "I'm wasting these people's time, this is ridiculous." I phoned Jonathan and told him to go to M&S [Marks & Spencer department store] and get me some new pyjamas. I thought it was all a fuss about nothing.

Finding the Worst

The next morning I had an ultrasound. The radiographer had a student with her, and, as she looked at my left side, she was explaining to him what she could see on the screen; then she moved to my right side and went quiet. I heard her say "mass," and "vascular." I asked what she meant, but she was noncommittal: she could see something, so she was sending me for a CT scan. I had this dawning realisation: that's a £500 scan, they're not going to do that lightly; there's something really wrong here.

When the consultant gynaecologist came to see me, she was straight up. "This is not good news. We've found a mass on your right ovary. It's about 11cm, and it looks solid. The swelling is coming from fluid, and that's not a great sign." She didn't say "cancer", but I knew that's what she meant. She asked if I had any kids. Jonathan and I have been together for about eight years and we'd decided we didn't want children, but what she told me was still a shock. "You're going to need a radical hysterectomy—uterus, ovaries, everything." I started howling. "But I don't feel unwell. I go running." It's strange, but you have an image of yourself as a healthy person. She said: "Look, it's not curtains. We're going to do whatever we can." And as soon as she said that, I

> **FAST FACT**
>
> Data compiled by the National Cancer Institute found that from 2004 to 2008, just 7.3 percent of all ovarian cancer cases were found in women aged thirty-five to forty-four.

thought: "That means it is curtains. This is terrible." As soon as I could, I got on the net and looked at the stats: 6,600 new cases each year—and 4,300 deaths. Then I really did think: "Oh hell, I'm dead now."

I had surgery a week later. It was only when they removed the tumour that they could give me a definitive diagnosis. When the oncology surgeon said, "I'm very sorry, Jennifer, but it's malignant: it is cancer," Jonathan fainted. I felt so sorry for him. There he was, on the floor, surrounded by three gorgeous nurses, and I'm sitting there in bed, thinking: "Hey, this is my moment. Attention on me, please."

Surviving Treatment

That was the bad news, but the good news was that my cancer was at an early stage (stage I), and it was confined to the ovary, though it was very aggressive grade 3. The hysterectomy was incredibly painful, but the chemo wasn't as bad as I'd expected. Yes, you feel hellish, but then you get on and do stuff.

My hair started corning out like candyfloss after my first treatment, so Jonathan shaved off the rest. I used to be really vain about it: I had permanent straightening, which cost half a month's salary, but I loved my sleek, shiny locks. When I lost it, I bought a couple of fab wigs, the hair I'd always wanted. I must sound like a prima donna, but it's the trivial things you hang onto. It's a coping mechanism. And the clothes, the hair, they're part of our identity as women.

I wasn't over the moon to go into surgical menopause at the age of 40. I've put on about 1½ stones [21 pounds], and I don't have a waist any more. My temperature has gone bananas, too, so I have hot flushes. You just don't function the way a 40-year-old should, and that's hard. I can't take HRT [hormone replacement therapy] to lessen the symptoms because that feeds the cancer—my tumour was oestrogen-receptive. Get cancer and put on weight: how lucky can you be?

It was only after I finished chemo that I really did go down that black hole of thinking: "Oh, my God, I'm going to die. I've got so many things to do yet." After counselling, though, I saw it differently. I do still whinge [complain] about the trivial, but it bothers me much less. It's such a cliché, but I get so much pleasure out of small things now. And with work, I'm like, "So what?" I don't stress about it. The world will go on.

As women, we tend to ignore certain physical symptoms, but if something's bothering you, go and see your GP about it. You're not wasting their time.

GLOSSARY

CT scan (abdominal)	A series of abdominal X-rays that are used to detect masses on the ovary.
adjuvant therapy	Chemotherapy given to ovarian cancer patients after their tumors have been removed. *See* neoadjuvant therapy.
alternative therapies	Medical practices that fall outside the conventional treatments prescribed by doctors. Alternative treatments are sometimes used in addition to prescribed medicine, for example, to reduce pain or anxiety.
ascites	An abnormal accumulation of fluid in the abdominal cavity; in women with ovarian cancer, the fluid may contain free-floating cancer cells.
benign tumor	A noncancerous growth consisting of cells that reproduce uncontrollably but do not spread to other tissues.
biopsy	The removal of a small sample of tissue for examination under a microscope; used for the diagnosis of cancer and to check for infection.
carcinogen	Any substance capable of causing cancer by mutating a cell's DNA.
chemotherapy	Treatment with various combinations of chemicals or drugs, particularly for the treatment of cancer.
clinical trial	The procedure of testing a new drug for safety and effectiveness in treating a particular disease or condition. Clinical trials are carried out under strict controls to assure the most accurate results. The US Food and Drug Administration uses these trials as the basis for its decision on whether or not to approve a drug.

debulking surgery	Excision of a major part of a malignant tumor that cannot be entirely removed; performed to enhance the effectiveness of follow-up radiation therapy or chemotherapy.
epithelial ovarian cancer	Ovarian cancer that is derived from the surface of the ovary. It is the most common form of ovarian cancer.
germ cell ovarian cancer	Ovarian cancer that is derived from the egg-producing cells inside the ovary. It is more common in teens and children than in adult women.
imaging techniques	Tests that help doctors locate a tumor even if it is deep in the body. These tests include magnetic resonance imaging and computed tomography scans, among others.
laparotomy	A surgical incision of the abdomen.
malignant	A term used to describe tumor cells that can spread to invade and destroy other tissues and organs.
metastasis	The spread of cancerous cells from one part of the body to another, often through blood or lymphatic vessels.
mutation	Changes to the DNA of a cell caused by mistakes during cell division or damage from environmental agents. Mutations can be harmful, beneficial, or insignificant. Some genetic mutations interfere with the regulation of cell division and can lead to cancer.
neoadjuvant chemotherapy	Chemotherapy given to patients before the main treatment, such as surgery, in the hopes of shrinking the tumor and improving the odds of survival.
oncology	The branch of medicine that diagnoses and treats cancer.
oophorectomy	The surgical removal of an ovary.
pathologist	A doctor who studies and diagnoses diseases by examining cells and tissues under a microscope.
pelvic exam	A medical examination of the organs of the female reproductive system.

prognosis A prediction of the outcome of cancer, ovarian or otherwise, based on stage at diagnosis and data collected from thousands of other patients.

radiation therapy A treatment that uses radiation to kill cancer cells. Radiation therapy can be used in lieu of surgery to destroy a tumor or in conjunction with surgery and/or chemotherapy. Radiation can be externally applied or taken internally as pellets or liquid.

rectovaginal pelvic exam A procedure in which a physician examines the ovaries through the rectum and vagina.

remission The state in which evidence and symptoms of cancer have decreased or disappeared. This state may be temporary or permanent.

staging The use of various diagnostic methods to determine accurately the extent of ovarian and other cancers. Staging is used to select the appropriate type and amount of treatment and to predict the outcome of treatment.

CHRONOLOGY

1960s   Alkylating agents—which prevent cancerous cells from reproducing by disrupting their DNA strands—are discovered. The main line of defense against ovarian cancer, these agents are a combination of chemotherapy drugs; the five-year survival rate following treatment is about 7 percent.

1971   The National Cancer Act is signed into law, creating the National Cancer Program for the continuing treatment of all cancers.

1978   Cisplatin, a chemotherapy drug, is approved by the US Food and Drug Administration (FDA) for the treatment of testicular and ovarian cancers; the first combination chemotherapy is developed, which is shown to extend patient life spans by as much as a year over single-use chemotherapy; however, the side effects of this potent cocktail are severe for some women.

Early 1980s   Several studies prove that birth control pills are effective in preventing ovarian cancer.

Mid-1980s   Multiple studies reveal that elevated levels of the protein CA-125 can indicate the presence of ovarian cancer; however, other conditions such as menstruation and pregnancy can cause high levels of CA-125 as well.

1992   Paclitaxel, a chemotherapy agent developed by the National Cancer Institute, is approved by the FDA for the treatment of many cancers, including ovarian cancer; it is found to shrink tumors by more than one-half, even in women whose cancers had become resistant to treatment.

Late 1990s Researchers discover that mutations of the BRCA1 and BRCA2 genes increase a woman's risk of developing ovarian cancer by more than 80 percent.

1999 The FDA approves the drug liposomal doxorubicin to treat therapy-resistant ovarian cancer; it is delivered directly to the cancer site, which limits its side effects and harm to other organs.

2005 The Cancer Genome Atlas Project is launched by the National Cancer Institute; the goal is to uncover specific genes that cause cancer, including ovarian cancer.

2006 The National Cancer Institute encourages doctors to discuss combining intraperitoneal chemotherapy— chemotherapy administered directly into the abdomen— with intravenous chemotherapy to extend the life spans of their patients by at least one year over intravenous chemotherapy alone.

2008 Oxford University epidemiologists conclusively prove that birth control pills lower the risk of ovarian cancer, going so far as to report in their article in the *Lancet* that more than thirty thousand women are saved each year due to the use of oral contraceptives.

2010 A study published in the September 1 issue of the *Journal of the American Medical Association* proves that women with the BRCA genes associated with ovarian cancer are less likely to develop the disease if their fallopian tubes and ovaries are removed.

ORGANIZATIONS TO CONTACT

The editors have compiled the following list of organizations concerned with the issues debated in this book. The descriptions are derived from materials provided by the organizations. All have publications or information available for interested readers. The list was compiled on the date of publication of the present volume; the information provided here may change. Be aware that many organizations take several weeks or longer to respond to inquiries, so allow as much time as possible.

American Association for Cancer Research (AACR)
615 Chestnut St., 17th Fl., Philadelphia, PA 19106
(215) 440-9300
fax: (215) 440-9313
e-mail: aacr@aacr.org
website: www.aacr.org

The mission of the AACR, founded in 1907, is to prevent and cure cancer through research, education, communication, and collaboration. The AACR website provides links to information about cancer in all forms, including a broad collection of articles on ovarian cancer. In addition to publishing seven major cancer journals, the AACR publishes *CR*, a magazine for cancer survivors, doctors, and scientists, and hosts major conventions that focus on current cancer research.

American Cancer Society (ACS)
250 Williams St. NW
Atlanta, GA 30303
(800) 227-2345
website: www.cancer.org

The ACS is a nationwide, community-based voluntary health organization dedicated to eliminating cancer as a major health problem. The ACS website maintains an exhaustive collection of resources dedicated to ovarian cancer and other cancers. In addition to fact sheets, the website includes the brochures *Ovarian Cancer: Detailed Guide* and *Ovarian Cancer: Overview Guide.*

Centers for Disease Control and Prevention (CDC)
1600 Clifton Rd.
Atlanta, GA 30333
(800) 232-4636
e-mail: cdcinfo@cdc
.gov
website: www.cdc.gov

Founded in 1946, the CDC helps communities protect the well-being of their citizens through health promotion; prevention of disease, injury, and disability; and preparedness for new health threats. In addition to pages on hundreds of other diseases, the CDC maintains a web page that focuses on ovarian cancer, including basic information and links to current research conducted by the CDC on the disease. Recent studies include "How Are Symptoms of Ovarian Cancer Managed? A Study of Primary Care Physicians" and "Gynecologic Oncologists and Ovarian Cancer Treatment: Avenues for Improved Survival."

Foundation for Women's Cancer (FWC)
230 W. Monroe St.
Ste. 2528, Chicago, IL
60606
(312) 578-1439
fax: (312) 578-9769
e-mail: info@founda
tionforwomenscancer
.org
website: www.founda
tionforwomenscancer
.gov

Formerly the Gynecologic Cancer Foundation, the FWC is a consolidation of the Women's Cancer Network, National Cervical Cancer Public Education Program, and the National Race to End Women's Cancer. Its core mission is to increase awareness and education, support expanded research and training, and provide knowledge and hope for women diagnosed with cancers specific to them. The FWC website is a clearinghouse for information about ovarian cancer, including brochures and fact sheets such as "Ovarian Cancer Information" and "Sexuality."

Gilda Radner Familial Ovarian Cancer Registry
Roswell Park Cancer Institute, Elm and Carlton Sts., Buffalo NY 14263
(800) 682-7426
website: http://ovarian
cancer.org

The Gilda Radner Familial Ovarian Cancer Registry has amassed data on more than forty-five hundred women who have been diagnosed with ovarian cancer in more than 1,850 families in which two or more members have ovarian cancer. The registry's website contains important information about the disease, including current discoveries concerning the genetic causes of ovarian cancer. In addition to fact sheets, website visitors can read the yearly newsletter and the latest research reports.

National Cancer Institute (NCI)
6116 Executive Blvd.
Ste. 300, Bethesda, MD 20892-8322
(800) 422-6237
website: www.cancer
.gov

A division of the National Institutes of Health, the NCI coordinates the National Cancer Program, which conducts and supports research, training, health information dissemination, and other programs with respect to the cause, diagnosis, prevention, and treatment of cancer; rehabilitation from cancer; and the continuing care of cancer patients and the families of cancer patients. The NCI website maintains an extensive portal of information about ovarian cancer. Visitors can read about the results of clinical trials, the latest developments in cancer drugs, and other reports, such as "Menopausal Hormone Replacement" and "Snapshot of Ovarian Cancer."

National Comprehensive Cancer Network (NCCN)
275 Commerce Dr., Ste. 300, Fort Washington, PA 19034
(215) 690-0300
fax: (215) 690-0280
website: www.nccn
.com

The NCCN, a not-for-profit alliance of twenty-one of the world's leading cancer centers, is dedicated to improving the quality and effectiveness of care provided to patients with cancer. The NCCN's website offers an extensive collection of information about ovarian cancer and other cancers as well. In addition to many informative videos, the website provides articles and studies, including "How to React to an Abnormal Pap Smear Result" and "Early Detection Key in Ovarian Cancer."

National Ovarian Cancer Coalition (NOCC)
2501 Oak Lawn Ave. Ste. 435, Dallas, TX 75219
(888) 682-7426
fax: (214) 273-4201
website: www.ovarian
.org

Through national programs and local chapter initiatives, the NOCC's goal is to make more people aware of the early symptoms of ovarian cancer. In addition, the NOCC provides information to assist the newly diagnosed patient, to provide hope to survivors, and to support caregivers. The coalition's website provides informational videos, pamphlets, and brochures about the disease, including "When a Loved One Has Ovarian Cancer" and "Woman to Woman."

Ovarian Cancer Institute (OCI)
960 Johnson Ferry Rd. Ste. 130, Atlanta, GA 30342
(404) 300-2997
fax: (404) 300-2986
e-mail: elizabeth@ovariancancerinstitute.org
website: http://ovariancancerinstitute.org

The primary mission of the OCI is to develop innovative research leading to earlier detection and more effective treatment of ovarian cancer as well as to educate and heighten awareness of the symptoms of ovarian cancer and treatment options. Currently, the OCI Laboratories have almost six hundred tumor samples available for research. In addition to research summaries, the OCI website provides informative videos and fact sheets about ovarian cancer, including "Using Magnetic Nanoparticles to Attack Cancer Cells."

Ovarian Cancer National Alliance (OCNA)
901 E St. NW, Ste. 405 Washington, DC 20004
(202) 331-1332
fax: (202) 331-2292
e-mail: ocna@ovariancancer.org
website: www.ovariancancer.org

The OCNA advocates at a national level for increases in research funding for the development of an early detection test, improved health care practices, and lifesaving treatment protocols. In addition, the alliance educates health care professionals and raises public awareness of the risks, signs, and symptoms of ovarian cancer. In addition to a comprehensive resources guide, the OCNA website contains links to the alliance's monthly newsletter and to the *Teal Journal*, webinars, and fact sheets.

FOR FURTHER READING

Books

American Cancer Society, *QuickFACTS: Advanced Cancer.* Atlanta, GA: American Cancer Society, 2008.

Chris Bledy, *Beating Ovarian Cancer: How to Overcome the Odds and Reclaim Your Life.* Harrison, NY: Book Clearing House, 2008.

Kathryn Carter and Laurie Elit, eds., *Bearing Witness: Living with Ovarian Cancer.* Waterloo, ON: Wilfrid Laurier University Press, 2009.

Cheryl Cushine, *The Dust Busting Chronicles: Cleaning My Way Through Ovarian Cancer.* Bloomington, IN: Authorhouse, 2007.

Giuseppe Del Priore and J. Richard Smith, *Women's Cancers: Pathways to Healing; A Patient's Guide to Dealing with Ovarian and Breast Cancer.* New York: Springer, 2008.

Sue Friedman, Rebecca Sutphen, and Kathy Steligo, *Confronting Hereditary Breast and Ovarian Cancer: Identify Your Risk, Understand Your Options, Change Your Destiny.* Baltimore, MD: Johns Hopkins University Press, 2012.

Victoria Zacheis Greve and Karen Greve Young, *Love You So Much: A Mother and Daughter's Shared Memoir; Breaking the Silence of Ovarian Cancer from Across the Miles.* London: Summertime, 2011.

Carole McCaskill, *What Color Is My Ribbon? An Ovarian Cancer Success Story.* Bloomington, IN: Xlibris, 2011.

Joi L. Morris and Ora K. Gordon, *Positive Results: Making the Best Decisions When You're at High Risk for Breast or Ovarian Cancer.* Amherst, NY: Prometheus, 2010.

Ritu Saiani and Robert E. Bristow, *Johns Hopkins Medicine Patients' Guide to Ovarian Cancer.* Sudbury, MA: Jones and Bartlett, 2011.

Periodicals and Internet Sources

Melinda Beck, "Toward Earlier Detection of Ovarian Cancer," *Wall Street Journal*, August 4, 2009.

Christopher Dolinsky and Carolyn Vachani, "Ovarian Cancer: The Basics," OncoLink, Abramson Cancer Center of the University of Pennsylvania, January 14, 2012. www.oncolink.org /types/article.cfm?c=6&s=19&ss=766&id=8589&p=1.

Andrew E. Green and Jules E. Harris, "Ovarian Cancer," Medscape Reference: Drugs, Diseases, and Procedures. http://emedi cine.medscape.com/article/255771-overview.

Beth Hahn, "Nurse Shares Story About Fight Against Ovarian Cancer," *Reporter*, October 27, 2012.

Melissa Healy, "Ovarian Cancer Risk Increases After IVF," *Los Angeles Times*, October 27, 2011.

Katherine Hobson, "Prostate, Ovarian Cancer Screening: When to Test? Not So Clear," *US News & World Report*, March 18, 2009.

Patricia Jasen, "From the 'Silent Killer' to the 'Whispering Disease': Ovarian Cancer and the Uses of Metaphor," *Medical History*, October 2009.

Christine Lennon, "Ovarian Cancer: Fighting for a Cure," *Harper's Bazaar*, June 3, 2009.

Fiona Macrae, "Ovarian Cancer Hope as 'Killer' Gene Discovered," *Mail Online*, August 3, 2009. www.dailymail.co.uk /health/article-1203922/Ovarian-cancer-hope-killer-gene -discovered.html.

Memorial Sloan-Kettering Cancer Center, "Ovarian Cancer." www.mskcc.org/cancer-care/adult/ovarian.

New Scientist, "Ovarian Cancer Cells 'Bully' Their Way to Other Organs," June 18, 2011.

Christian Nordqvist, "What Is Ovarian Cancer? What Causes Ovarian Cancer?," Medical News Today, August 4, 2009. www .medicalnewstoday.com/articles/159675.php.

Alice Park, "Ovarian Cancer Screening: Hope for Early Detection," *Time*, May 20, 2010.

Rebecca Smith, "Obesity Raises Risk of Ovarian Cancer," *Daily Telegraph* (London), January 4, 2009.

Jeannine Stein, "Diet May Play a Part in Ovarian Cancer Survival Rates," *Network Journal*, March 5, 2010.

Jennipher Walters, "The Pill Cuts the Risk of Ovarian Cancer," *Shape*, October 27, 2011.

Catherine Winters, "How to Protect Yourself from Ovarian Cancer," *Prevention*, November 2011. www.prevention.com /health/health-concerns/ovarian-cancer-prevention-and -diagnosis.

INDEX